Out Of Latvia

Out Of Latvia

A Latvian Immigrant's Son Searches for his Roots

The story of Peter Jirgens,
written by David Kerr

Foreword

I met Peter Jirgens in March 2013 on a charity bicycle ride from Sydney to Mt Kosciuszko. For three nights Peter kept our group spellbound as he recounted the story of his risky mission into Latvia and daring hitchhiking adventures throughout Europe. Each night, crammed into a cabin in our lodgings in Jindabyne, we eagerly awaited the next instalment of Peter's amazing tale. As I listened and watched the faces of my cycling colleagues, I knew this was a story the world needed to hear, and I pleaded with Peter to allow me to write it. I am very grateful for the privilege to share the story of this generous, creative, and likeable Aussie.

David Kerr

Contents

Illustrations

Part 1

Chapter One - The Early Years

"We shall not cease from exploration
And the end of all our exploring
Will be to arrive where we started
And know the place for the first time."
T. S. Eliot, *Four Quartets*

Heavy silence blankets the room. I look out of the window. In the street below, the traffic flows past with monotonous regularity. It's obscene how the world continues its rhythm while Dad loses his battle to live. I turn to my brother, John, standing beside me. Our eyes meet for an instant before he returns his gaze to our father. The hospital staff called us earlier and we made the journey from Nowra to Wollongong in record time.

When we arrived, the nurse said, "He's fading fast. He's fought so hard, but he's running out of strength. I suspect he wants to see you before he goes."

Now we stand in a private room typical of any hospital: clinical, white sheets, heart monitor, intravenous stand and two grey padded chairs. Dad's skin is pasty grey. The bloodstained cannula in his hand provides him with pain-free life, flowing from the transparent bag suspended beside his bed. The smell of death surrounds us.

"John," I say, "I'll wait outside and give you some time alone."

John nods, and I walk to the door and close it quietly. Mum and my sister Julie could not be present. They said their good-byes yesterday. John and I have the painful privilege of our final farewell to father.

Minutes later, the door swings open and John steps out, his eyes moist and face drained of colour. I enter the sacred space with a heavy heart. Dad's eyes, glazed, lifeless, signal death's imminence. I wonder if he's already dead.

"I love you, Dad. Thanks for all you've done for us, for me, over the years. You've provided so well for us, and I'm so grateful. I love you, Dad." I spoke sincerely, straight from the heart. I meant it.

Suddenly, life returns to his eyes. I take his huge limp hand — Jirgen's men all have huge hands. These bear the marks of a thousand stories, stories of courage, hardship and survival, stories of risk and deception, stories of failure and hope. His eyes close again, and I know he's gone. He has taken his last breath. I stare in disbelief, shocked. Tears spill down my cheeks. I dreaded this day, and now it has finally arrived.

"I love you, Dad," I whisper, though it was not always true.

* * *

The finished job stands before us. Relief and sadness mark John's face. Perspiration drips from his unshaven chin.

"I guess we should try it," he says.

Mum appears at the door of the garage, wiping her hands on a well-worn apron. She'd regularly checked our progress during the day, and John and I agreed it was important to include her in our treasured project. Before us sits our black, marine-ply masterpiece. It will carry Dad to his final resting place.

I look at her, pause for a moment, then gesture to the casket. "Would you mind helping us out?" Mum is a similar size to Dad.

She hesitates and eyes me with concern.

"It's okay, Mum," I assure her.

She walks over and steps gingerly into our work of art. Slowly, she lowers herself, gripping the sides of the casket to support the weight of her body. Once seated, she shuffles forward until her feet touch the end of the casket, then she lies back, resting on the hard base.

"A perfect fit," I say with relief.

The casket is now complete. I lean forward and gently take Mum's wrinkled hand. John kneels on the opposite side, his large, suntanned hands supporting Mum's elbow, and slowly we lift her to her feet.

"Well done, boys. Your father would be most impressed." She turns and walks towards the door, her eyes filling with tears. "I'll make some tea, and I've baked some scones for you."

I glance down. My tears, mingled with perspiration, have pooled on the floor. We've not stopped since early morning, and my body, drained of energy, cries out for respite.

Twenty-four hours had passed since Dad died, and recent weeks had been an emotional roller coaster. Two weeks earlier, I'd given the casting vote to remove his left leg. The toxins in Dad's body required drugs, but the drugs caused hallucinations. The doctor believed he was incapable of making a rational decision and had pressed the family for a decision. The surgeon had removed his left leg twelve months earlier because of the onset of gangrene. The insidious disease had progressively overtaken his right leg. Julie, my sister, voted to remove his leg; John, for keeping it intact; and Mum abstained. There was no other real alternative, so off it came. Sadly, it didn't save him. I find it unbelievable that his body, once strong and active, is now lifeless.

John and I created Dad's coffin with the few remaining tools Dad had bought for 500 pounds to build a timber bridge when we lived at Lake Cargelligo, near Urana. This remote environment became home for Mum and Dad after he migrated from Latvia in 1949. The tools had seen better days. John and I had used and misused them in our childhood, trying to cultivate the skills of our father. He could do anything—a clever "Jack-of-all-Trades". He taught us well. These instruments were now precious. Once held by his large, rough hands, they had created a life and a future for us.

During the final stages of completing our labour of love, I'd discovered the lid of the coffin was two millimetres out of alignment. "What should we do?" I'd asked John, and I knew the answer before I'd added, "What would Dad say?"

We started from scratch again. This toil was in honour of our father, so it had to be to his standard. It was our final tribute to him, using his tools and the skills he had patiently modelled over the years.

Tools and artefacts collected over a lifetime cover the walls of the fibro garage, silent witnesses to our sacred task. The rich aroma of tobacco lingers in the air. Dad, a pensioner, grew his own tobacco to save money. Often we had to fight our way through dozens of tobacco plants hanging from the ceiling. Bottles of his distinctive home brew, carefully concocted from his secret recipe, line the shelves.

The black marine ply reflects the late afternoon sun, and the light draws me back to my task. I show John the two chrome roof racks I'd found. "How about we fit them to each side of the casket?"

John smiles and nods his approval.

We've already attached a chromed display window from an old petrol bowser. It used to show the price and quantity of petrol, but now, at John's suggestion, it shows a photo of Dad.

14

I glance around Dad's garage again and spot a large door-knocker on a shelf—the 'piece de resistance'. I reach up, take it my hand and smile. "How about we fix this to the front of the casket?" I suggest, holding it out. "It'll help St Peter gain Dad's attention when he arrives at the Pearly Gates."

John grins. His large, rough hands fix the knocker to the front, and I mount a shiny grill at the other end.

* * *

That day will stay with me forever, a labour of love with my brother. Our best efforts to distinguish a man who fearlessly faced every challenge life repeatedly, and often unkindly, flung at him.

Our family was chiselled from granite formed by the powerful forces and turbulence of early Eastern European history, and the more recent cruelty of a Communist regime. The beauty and resilience of Baltic amber symbolize Latvia. Hidden in the soil, washed in the sea, petrified by the process of time into something which in early days was more precious than gold. Like gold, it can hold heat and be shaped into jewellery coveted by women worldwide.

Dad escaped from Latvia after World War II. He originally served with the Russians, then moved across to the German Army where he worked in the transport division. Six months after the war began, he was required to transport material to Riga and took the opportunity to call in on his family. There he discovered from a neighbour they had planned to leave by boat for the safety of Sweden. Later, he heard that the Russians had bombed boats crossing the Baltic Sea, and he wondered if his family had survived. He wrote to his mother many times, hoping his letters would find her, but after ten years without a response, he assumed that she, and other members of the family, had perished crossing the Baltic Sea. At the age of twenty-seven, Dad moved to Australia.

15

The Australian Government required Dad to work for two years to pay for his passage, and they used his skills in the construction of Warragamba Dam. Later, he moved to Innisvale, where he cut sugar cane. He met my mother in Manila, near Tamworth; they married in Melbourne, then returned to Urana but moved again when Dad was contracted to build a wooden bridge at Lake Cargelligo.

In 1954, Dad, wanting to escape the harsh heat of outback New South Wales, bought a block of ground, unseen, at Waterpark Road, St Georges Basin, 190 kilometres south of Sydney. He travelled by train to Bomaderry to inspect the property, but when he asked a taxi driver to take him to his new acquisition, the driver replied, "No roads in that area."

Though shocked, Dad knew it wasn't the end of the world. He went back to Lake Cargelligo, collected his family and moved to the coastal town of Nowra. Unsure of where to live or what to do, Dad struck up a conversation with a bloke he found building his own house in Kinghorne Street. The conversation led to Dad helping him finish his home, and eventually they worked together building caravans. The builder sold Dad a block at the top of the hill in Kinghorne Street, and that's where he built our home.

* * *

My mother came from Irish stock. My sister, Julie, traced Mum's roots back to County Antrim in the north-eastern corner of Ireland and discovered that she's related to Ellen Quinn, mother of the iconic Australian bushranger, Ned Kelly. It appears I have a rich mixture of blood in my veins!

Beginning a new life in Nowra created a challenge for the family. I don't remember the move—I was only one year old! At first, we stayed in Ryan's Caravan Park, then Dad built a garage on the Kinghorne Street property, and we lived in that for six years until he completed our home. It was cramped, living in

16

such a small space. However, the biggest challenge was the isolation of living out of town. Our few neighbours were scattered through the bush. It took time to make friends, but they became great friends—we did everything together. In 1956, Dad bought a six-ton Dodge truck and mined the sand-hills at Shoalhaven Heads. Mining was a simple but exhausting process. Dad stood beside his vehicle and shovelled six tonne of sand over the high sides of the truck—strenuous, backbreaking work, made worse by summer heat. Up to three loads of sand travelled along that track every day, supplying local and commercial construction. The Paper Mill was being built at the time, which increased demand for the construction of homes for workers.

Dad's truck often became bogged. On one occasion near the Paper Mill, the truck sank up to its axles in mud under the weight of a full load of sand. The only way to free the old beast was to tip the load onto the track and shovel out by hand whatever remained. With the truck empty, Dad opened the driver's door, depressed the accelerator with his left hand and, with his shoulder against the doorpost, pushed the truck free. Then, racing against time to meet the deadlines of his clients, he returned to the sand hills, shovelled new sand over the high sides of the old truck and then drove out again, skilfully manoeuvring past the site of the earlier unloading.

Dad bought a second truck in 1960, an International, the first diesel truck in Nowra. He hired it out to locals and the Shoalhaven Council. Unfortunately, he found it difficult to get work because some locals regarded him as a 'wog'. On a typical day, when Dad came home in the evening Mum would ask, "How did you go today?"

Dad shook his head. "Hung around council depot 'til ten o'clock. Rest of locals managed to get jobs. None for me."

Mum's face crinkled with concern and disappointment. "Again," she stammered.

I don't know how Dad managed to put food on the table. A

number of council employees didn't like him, and he only got jobs nobody else wanted. These 'mountain runs' required more fuel and increased wear and tear on the vehicle. The 'exclusive club' was not going to let a 'Latvian wog' onto their turf. I felt sad for Dad and wanted to make things right for him. But what could a kid do?

As time passed, I became increasingly angry at the way these people treated Dad. Every abusive comment, every rejection he suffered because of his nationality, felt like a stab wound in my chest. I didn't understand how people could be so cruel, but I hid my anger and hurt from my parents and from friends. Generally, my mates accepted me, and I tried as best I could to win their friendship. Being good at sport impressed Aussie eyes, and I worked hard to be the best I could be. I guess it worked.

A change of fortune came in 1964—a discovery that held great promise. Dad found a large outcrop of rock in bush land on the outskirts of Milton. Over two years he built a crusher out of anything he could find which fitted his visionary blueprint. To help the cash flow during its construction, Dad made septic tanks, mixing concrete by hand, and delivering them to locals. He mixed the concrete for 6,000 litre tanks and poured it into steel moulds. A block and tackle on an 'A wooden frame' construction anchored to the back of the International helped him raise the tank onto the truck. He managed the entire operation without help. He was a one man operator, creative, and determined.

The plant was huge, about the size of two houses. Contracts to supply road base, concrete and sealing aggregate to the local council soon rewarded his initiative. I remember the day he proudly drove into Milton with the first load of crushed metal. Dad's hard work and determination had won him some mates, and they hauled him into the pub for celebratory drinks.

However, his success was short-lived. Dad's unscrupulous bank manager saw Dad's success and formed an alliance with twelve businessmen, who each put in 1,000 pounds. They developed a similar crusher, deliberately undercutting Dad's price below cost for twelve months. Growing debt forced him out of business. Determined not to apply for bankruptcy, he made the tough decision to repay his debts. He dismantled the crusher and sold the parts. He could have built three houses with the money he spent on its construction. Dad never recovered from that bitter blow. I watched him struggle through those cruel months, and I went with him to the quarry and helped him dismantle the crusher. The process of demolishing his unique creation was painful. A sad silence sat uncomfortably with us in the cabin of the truck every time we went to the quarry. The crusher had been his pride and joy, so cleverly assembled, one of a kind. Many of the components were sold to help cover his losses. Life was tough for him and also for us.

In ongoing attempts to repay his debts, he travelled to the Riverina for eight years and took on earth-moving jobs. Dad never gave up, and he finally paid off his debts. He was a man of principle. He did right by people and they came to respect him.

The discrimination Dad suffered by council staff and the dishonesty of his bank manager did not create a positive view of Australia for Dad. Though he lived in Australia, his heart was in Latvia. He regularly received the *Baltic News*, an underground newspaper that kept him in touch with the latest happenings in his homeland. He longed to return. It was always on his mind.

One day, when Mum was reading the latest *Baltic News*, she said, "Arnold, it says here that two Latvians recently returned to Latvia from America and have not been heard of since. I don't want you to even think of going back. It's too dangerous."

He knew of other Latvians who hadn't been able to resist reconnecting with their much-loved land and had disappeared without trace. Dad said he would return, but not while the Soviet Communists occupied his country. The Australian government granted him permanent residency and the local council accepted it. However, when it came to the official ceremony where council members would be present, he said, "I will not stand before the councillors who have deliberately ruined my business." He also did not like the idea of pledging allegiance to the Queen.

If he returned to Latvia while still classified as Latvian, he would be liable to be called up for service in the Soviet Army, or, possibly worse, be sent to Siberia.

Chapter Two - The School of Hard Knocks

*"He who knows no hardships will know no hardihood. He
who faces no calamity will need no courage. Mysterious
though it is, the characteristics in human nature which we
love best grow in a soil with a strong mixture of troubles."*
Harry Emerson Fosdick

I loved hearing Dad tell stories of his family and youth. Sometimes on a Saturday night after dinner, I would ask him to tell us about Latvia. He would lie back in his old armchair, a beer within reach, and transport us back to his beloved country. Those times are indelibly etched on my mind. His memories settled in my mind and gradually created hunger. One powerful story featured my grandmother and Uncle John. Dad spoke English reasonably well but always with a thick accent. Often he would leave words out or misplace them. I had to concentrate to understand what he was saying.

"In 1947, your grandmother and uncle transported to Siberia in railway carriages—more like cattle trucks. Russian troops taken from their home in Riga with force. They spent two weeks rolling across countryside, where open country was—no people settled—sleeping on straw on carriage floor in very bad conditions—no toilets. Doors finally opened and were pushed out into forest—nothing there, only trees. Later, they learn this was Soviet strategy to develop forest regions in central Siberia. Hundreds of thousands of people from cities and towns in Latvia taken by force and dumped in the forests and plains of Siberia."

Concerned, I asked, "How did they survive?"

Dad nodded as if he thought it a fair question. "On their first night in open air, dug hole with sticks — covered themselves with pine branches — shelter from cold. Everyone worked together with basic tools to build huts. Spent eight years there in forced labour. My mother chop wood to survive. If not produce full daily quota, she not get paid for that day. Your Uncle John — excellent hunter. He learn how to be furrier before war and soon had good living selling furs. After eight years, Uncle John came back to Riga, followed by my mother. She suffered bad frostbite and ... problems from being in open air from freezing winter temperatures. Latvian doctors said this made her white blood cells lower. She return to Riga when seventy years old and should have got pension and financial support for medicine to keep her alive. The Soviets told her she not meet necessary 'work years' in Latvia to get aged pension and then had to work 'til she is eighty. Her time in Siberia not count, even though she was moved against her will from her homeland." Dad paused and glanced at the floor. He was not one to show emotion and was working hard to keep his composure.

Anger rose in my chest. "That is so wrong — so unfair."

"Yes, my mother and brother aged terrible during those years. However, your uncle did well on return to Riga — managed food produce from farms owned by State. His skills and good ability helped him — became known and invited to become Communist Party member in Riga. Only twelve percent of population belonged to Communist Party. They enjoy privileges denied to 'the peasants'. However, John not accept any invitation connecting him with government that mistreat his people and his land so cruelly — violently. He refuse invitation. Soviets sent him back to Siberia to punish him. Also with 1600 young men. Sixteen

22

months later, he return to Riga with, I think, around 900 of the young men. 'If a guard not like you,' your uncle said, 'he took your blanket at night — next morning you were found dead.'" Dad's jaw tightened with anger. Other times when he spoke of these events, his eyes would moisten or his fingers would clench into fists.

Somehow Dad and my forbears survived those brutal days. These powerful forces shaped my family and forged the Latvian people into a solid united body, which has contributed to their resilience and helped preserve their rich culture. Dad was a chip off that rock. I had some fragments inside me, and I became fascinated with this country. Every time Dad brought his family to life with stories, I wanted to be with them. His cherished land was never far from my mind, and his heartbeat resonated within me. In my youth, I was more Latvian than Australian. I understood Dad's deep longing to return to his birthplace — his desire to sit with his mother in an armchair in the family home, laugh with brothers, play with his grandchildren and entertain neighbours with songs and music. An accomplished musician, Dad could play almost any instrument, including the saxophone, trumpet, clarinet, flute and piano accordion. He knew hundreds of folk songs. Every year Dad and thousands of Latvians from every region gathered in Riga for the Music Song and Dance Festival. The older I grew the stronger became my fascination and desire to visit the land of my forefathers. One day I would go and see it for myself.

* * *

I count myself fortunate to have grown up in the Shoalhaven, a region on the New South Wales south coast of which Nowra is the commercial hub. It is still one of the most beautiful and unspoilt parts of Australia's coastline. From Berry to North Durras, the ever-changing coastal landscape is a tapestry bathed in shimmering light, rich in natural beauty and alive with people of inspiration and character. The Shoalhaven takes in the coast, the fertile plains, the rugged mountain escarpment and the panoramic views of the eastern seaboard and embraces over 300,000 hectares of national parks and state forests, rivers, coastal lakes, estuaries and many miles of navigable waterways. Tourism is one of the main industries, and for many years, the thick forests yielded their red cedar for fine furniture and fittings. This was my playground during my youth and where I developed primitive construction skills and learned bushcraft.

I climbed the giant rocket in Bomaderry Park and chased mates around the iconic giant milk bottle outside Berry. In the early days of primary school, John, Julie and I used to build billy carts — usually an articulated arrangement with two seats, two wheels and the steering in the front, and a two-wheeled, four passenger cart connected to the rear. We lived on the highway on Brown's Hill, the highest hill in Nowra, and the only sealed road nearby was the Prince's Highway. The carts ran smoothly on this surface, enhanced by the use of old pram wheels on the hot bitumen seal. The only problem was the bend at the bottom which prevented the occupants of a cart descending at high speed from spotting an oncoming vehicle until it was too late. We posted a lookout on the bend to signal if any danger was present. We spent hours flying down that stretch of road.

Our expertise grew, and it wasn't long before we placed rocks at intervals on the centre of the road, providing a challenging slalom course. Negotiating the course at speed while watching the lookout and keeping balance on the cart required considerable skill. As time went on, we upgraded to ball-bearing wheels, which increased the speed significantly on smoother surfaces. There was more than one occasion when I screamed down the hill at breakneck speed, with kids hanging on, screeching, behind me, heading towards the bend at the bottom, and then saw the frantic signal from the lookout. I would swerve off the road in a spray of gravel as a semi-trailer roared past. We never told our parents about our favourite stretch on the highway.

* * *

While I loved the outdoors, I also enjoyed reading, especially the stories about King Arthur. My favourite is the legend about Prince Llywelyn, who was fond of hunting. Although he had many dogs, his favourite was Gelert, as he was fearless in the hunt and also a loyal friend and companion. One day Llewelyn and his wife went out hunting, leaving their baby son with a nurse and a servant to look after him. The nurse and the servant went for a walk in the mountains, leaving the baby alone and unprotected. Llewelyn was absorbed in his hunting, but after a while he noticed Gelert wasn't with the pack. The prince knew something was wrong as Gelert was always at the front of the hunt. He reasoned that the only place Gelert would go was back to the lodge, so he called off the hunt and headed back home. As the party dismounted, Gelert came running out of the lodge towards his master, covered in blood and wagging his tail. The princess, calling her child's name, fainted. Llewelyn rushed into the baby's room to find the cradle overturned, the bloodstained bedclothes thrown all over the floor and no sign of his son. Filled with anger and grief, he drew his sword and killed Gelert. As the dog died, his whimpers and cries were answered by the sound of a baby crying from behind the overturned cradle. Llewelyn pulled aside the cradle and found his son unharmed and the body of a huge wolf next to him. Gelert had killed the wolf as it tried to attack Llewelyn's son. With huge remorse, Llewelyn buried Gelert in a meadow nearby and marked his grave with a cairn of stones.

From an early age, travel books fascinated me, and the school library satisfied my hunger. The snow-covered mountains of Europe, the steamy tropics, the green meadows of England and Scotland reached out to me. The songs and dress of my Latvian family were familiar, but the cultures and customs of many countries captivated me. Night after night, I studied pictures of other nationalities and developed a desire to experience what I saw. One day I would go. Latvia was in my sights, but I also wanted to see the world.

Cubby houses were another cherished childhood activity. My friends John and Julie and I dug a hole in the ground three metres long, a metre wide and three quarters of a metre deep, and then covered it with boards, tin and a layer of soil on top. A tunnel several metres long formed the entranceway, the hole disguised by a large plate.

We also experimented with other types of construction. The bush provided small logs which we cut down and built walls log on log. On the first occasion, after erecting the roof, we realised we'd not provided for a door, so we dug a trench five or six metres away and covered it with hessian and carpet. To enter, you had to crawl in on hands and knees, avoiding the candles that lit up the tunnel.

Tree cubby houses were also part of our construction programme. I think we learned a great deal about the outdoors through being creative and working together. We felt at home in the bush. Also, I was good with a slingshot and could wipe out any birds at will, which I am not proud about today.

We made our own canoes and paddled them on a local watercourse called Brown's Creek. A sheet of corrugated iron formed the main structure. A piece of timber lay down the centre and lengths of timber inserted to separate the opening of the canoe in a V shape. To overcome the problem of leakage through the nail holes in the timber skeleton, we chipped bitumen away from the edge of a tarred road. The bitumen was heated over a small fire and applied to the holes. This usually took a full weekend and, when completed, the canoe was carted down to the water, at least half a kilometre, and ceremoniously launched. Half an hour later, after the joy of floating along the creek, it would invariably tip over and sink. Once on the bottom of the creek it could not be retrieved, so we walked back home to start again. In those days we were ignorant of outriggers, which would have been the answer to our problem of stability. I guess we made at least six canoes, and every one of them sank. In more recent times, with my kids and a young fellow I was mentoring, we built an outrigger with a couple of plastic drums, and that was a great success. Those early days were great entertainment and provided me with an education that city kids often miss. We loved the bush—we were part of the bush.

* * *

My entrepreneurial skills took root at an early age. We used to help pack up the annual Nowra show. Although mostly we were paid for our efforts, sometimes we worked for nothing. Behind our home where Shoalhaven High School is now located was a gun club. Shooters came every weekend and fired at clay pigeons. No houses existed there then, and spindly tussock grass covered the ground. Shooters often missed the clay pigeons. Some searched but couldn't find them because of the long grass, so after they finished shooting, John and I, with a few mates, would search through the long grass, find the unexploded clay pigeons and sell them back to the shooters for threepence each. One day, one of the shooters didn't pay me.

The next day I confronted his daughter and said, "Your father owes me money."

She scowled and threw herself at me. I fell to the ground beneath her weight—which was considerable—and we wrestled until I hit my head on a rock, then I burst into tears and scurried home. I was ten years old at the time, and to this day I've never been paid. Many years later, when I was in charge of road maintenance with the council, I met this guy again.

"Did you ever belong to the gun club at Nowra?" I asked.

"Yes,' he replied, eyes narrowing with suspicion.

I nodded but made no comment. He wanted the new roadway blended into his driveway, work he wasn't entitled to. I didn't do it. I guess that was rough justice.

* * *

Pain management was also a necessary part of my preparation for leaving the nest. One evening when I cycled home from football training, an oncoming car blinded me with their high beam as I approached a single lane bridge. I slowed down to let the approaching car cross ahead of me and then rode onto the bridge. Suddenly, a car struck me from behind and sent me over the rail into the creek, where I landed on top of my bike. I remember picking up my mangled bike and standing there, shocked and motionless, in the darkness with what appeared to be white stars falling out of my eyes. I had no idea what had happened. Then the picture became clear. Unfortunately, the dynamo powered by the rotation of my back wheel wasn't working, so I didn't have rear-lights. The oncoming car had also blinded the driver of the car, and she'd hit me. It took some time for the driver of the car, a Morris 1100, to approach me. She'd felt a bump but hadn't thought anything of it until she'd travelled a few kilometres up the road, then she decided to drive back and double check. I'm so glad she did. She found me standing beside the road, holding my bike with its twisted frame, buckled wheels and the pedal crank distorted to an angle of forty-five degrees. The only damage her car sustained was a broken front passenger blinker and snapped aerial. My right pedal had caught her blinker, and I'd hit the aerial and fallen over the railing on the bridge. I was grateful I'd gone over the rail—better than being sandwiched.

"How's your bike? Is your bike ok?" she asked.

"No," I gasped, then burst into tears.

The woman drove me home, and I sobbed every inch of the way. Mum opened the back door to find me soaked to the skin, bloodied, an emotional mess, and with the woman standing beside me. Mum talked with the woman, and they agreed that she would look after the repair to her car and I would take care of repairs to my bike. Repairs? My bike was a write-off! To add insult to injury that night, I lost my marbles—literally. I was good at marbles. I'm not sure if it was my large fingers, but over time I collected around 1,200. I started with two my cousin gave me and won the rest. The day of the accident, my skill had scored me no fewer than forty marbles, and they were in my school case securely strapped to a rack behind the seat of my bike. My suitcase sailed over the rail of the bridge with me, scattering my hard-earned winnings through the bush and into the creek. I returned to the scene a day later and only recovered four or five. That added more suffering to an already painful event.

My endless refinement in the crucible of suffering continued that year, 1967. I bought a beehive with John, a large colony of 50,000 bees, complete with smoker and net. We placed the hive under the eaves, out of direct sunlight, which was needed for best results. About four months later, I decided it was time to collect the honey. John was not around, and I thought I could manage the task without too many problems. I placed the ladder up against the side of the garage and stuffed rags into the smoker. After igniting it with a match, I gave it a few pumps. I pulled the net over my head and slipped on a pair of thin plastic gloves. Standing for a moment at the foot of the ladder, I mentally prepared myself for my first raid on the hive. I climbed the ladder, nervously removed the lid and poked the smoker into the hive. The bees responded on cue and remained calm. I slid one of the racks from the container, pulled a knife from my pocket and scraped the honey into the container—too easy. Then the unthinkable happened—the smoker went out.

Not to worry, I thought, *I'll just climb back down the ladder to where I'd left the matches and light the rags again.* I took one step down the ladder when a bee found its way under the hood and buzzed menacingly around my face. With the absence of smoke, the bees became more agitated. I made a decision, which in hindsight became my undoing. Intent on removing one bee, which was literally 'in my face', I didn't consider that one sting would be a thousand times better than having a colony of bees inject their barbs into me. A bee can only sting once, inflicting its pain, and then it dies. It's like a suicide bomber. Under stress, we don't always think rationally. That was the understatement of the moment. Off came the hood to remove the troublesome bee, and that signalled the colony to attack.

Whack.

Dozens of bees smacked into my face, injecting their stingers into my flesh. I screamed in agony, glanced down at the ground and decided that with hundreds of bees descending, the quickest way down was to jump. I leapt to the ground and screamed, "Open the door."

Mum heard the commotion and appeared at the door. She spotted me in full flight with the bees in hot pursuit and slammed the door shut and locked it. "You're not coming in here with those bees."

I took off and sprinted around the outside of the house with bees attacking my neck, arms, hands and legs, and even stinging between my fingers. I rolled on the grass, but they still kept coming at me. After completing a third circuit around the yard, I saw Mum standing behind the flyscreen door. She opened it. I rushed in and she slammed it behind me.

"Thanks Mum," I gasped.

Using a towel, Mum brushed away the bees fixed to my flesh and then proceeded to remove twenty-four stingers from my face and hands.

"Ouch, ouch, ouch!" My body screamed; it was on fire. I don't ever remember suffering as much physical pain as I did that afternoon.

I suspect that I'd removed many with my backyard antics in an attempt to dislodge the tormentors, but by nightfall, my face had swollen so much that I couldn't see. My ears, nose and lips looked grotesque, my hands so swollen that I'd lost the shape of my fingers. The ends of my arms felt like two great solid slabs of raw meat. With Dad away, we didn't have a car, and I couldn't cycle to the hospital because I couldn't see, so I had to suffer at home. The following day I missed school—one of the few times. Most of the bees survived, but I decided to give them away.

Accustomed to taking risks, I acquired my ability to live with danger at an early age. How could I not avoid the challenge of living on my wits? I was part of a migrant family and had a father whose nature and need for survival demanded that he 'live life on the edge'. Dad instilled in me a confidence and belief in myself from an early age, a vital preparation for my later adventures.

At eleven years of age, I worked in Dad's quarry on weekends. I helped him operate the seven tonne crusher, about the size of an average car. My main job, which I loved, was to blast the rock into smaller sizes after Dad had exploded it from the rock face. Dad drilled into the rock as far up as nineteen feet on the face. Then he filled the hole with ammonium nitrate and inserted a fuse with a detonator and gelignite. The spark from the plunger did the rest. While most of the exploded rock fitted into the crusher, and sledge-hammers broke up the smaller boulders—Dad went through boxes of sledge-hammer heads—boulders the size of car bodies remained. These were my job.

First, I'd drag the twenty kilo pneumatic drill and the heavy thirty millimetre air hoses into the quarry. At the blasting site, I'd drill a series of five holes, 150 millimetres deep. Then I dragged the drill and hoses out of the quarry to a safe distance to avoid damage from falling rocks. At first I considered it safer to drill and blast one hole at a time. However the physical effort of manhandling the equipment in and out of the quarry for a single blast was not efficient. Drilling and setting five charges was a more dangerous practice but worth the risk. Dad trained me well and trusted me.

The next part of the ritual was always dangerous. Returning to the blasting site, I'd insert a fuse into the detonator and clamp it. Then I'd push the detonator into the gelignite and place it in the hole. Every stick of gelignite had to explode. Dad warned me on many occasions that an unexploded stick, hidden under the debris, could prove fatal when he returned to the site with his mechanical loader to gather the fragmented rocks.

After that, I'd carefully calculate the length of fuse needed for each stick. Each charge needed to explode at roughly the same time. To ensure this happened, I'd vary the length of the fuse. The first charge lit would need the longest fuse, and I progressively shortened each of the following charges. I needed to ignite all the fuses in quick succession. Occasionally this didn't go to plan.

One of those days, when the sun hung high in the sky, I set the charges and lit the first two fuses. When I tried to strike the match for the third charge, it broke. I tried again and again, becoming progressively more desperate. I glanced back at the two fuses sizzling menacingly. Once lit, they never go out until they've done their work. Any attempt to extinguish them would result in failure. My heart raced. Time was running out. If I ran, three unexploded charges would remain buried under the rubble. Again I tried to light the match. Finally, the head burst into orange flame. I lit the third, fourth and fifth fuses, but could I reach my shelter before the first charge exploded? I raced towards the edge of the quarry, but it seemed unreachable. Adrenalin fuelled my legs, and I flew up the rise and around the perimeter at the top of the cutting. The first explosion ripped through the boulder when I was still metres from the rusted, upturned truck body I used as my 'bomb shelter.' Huge rocks flew high into the air. Then the second charge exploded. I threw myself into my shelter just as rocks the size of footballs smashed onto the truck, and the third, fourth and fifth explosions, blasting off in quick succession, brought further waves of jagged rocks. I lay in the dusty shelter of my refuge for some time, breathing heavily. It was a close call.

Dad asked me later if I'd had any problems.

"No, all went well," I replied. I never did tell Dad about this incident.

I wasn't going to confess any difficulties. I loved the job. Experiences like these equipped me to survive even greater danger during the mission I believe was part of my destiny. That mission had not yet formed fully in my young mind. All I knew at that age was that Latvia had captured my heart and the world was waiting for me.

Chapter Three - An Important Discovery

"People will not look forward to posterity,
who never look backward to their ancestors."
Edmund Burke

My education about aboriginals didn't come out of a textbook. My aboriginal friends taught me a great deal, and through their friendship I learned to accept people from cultures very different from my own — useful learning for my later adventures. My brother and I grew up with aboriginal people [1], and we always had a great respect for the original inhabitants of the land.

In my days as a rugby league player, my team included several Koori players. Every so often one would go 'walkabout', and I'd go and chase him up and try to get him back on the field. 'Tharawal', or 'Dharawal' as it is referred to in historical records, refers to the original peoples of the southern and south-western Sydney area. Their lands extend from the south side of Botany Bay, around Port Hacking to the north of the Shoalhaven River at Nowra and then inland to Campbelltown and Camden.

I'm amazed by their history and their intimate relationship with the land. Non-indigenous landowners might consider land as something they own, a commodity to be bought and sold, an asset to make a profit from, a means by which to make a living, or simply 'home'. For aboriginal people, the relationship is much deeper. The land owns Aboriginal people, and every aspect of their lives is connected to it. Aboriginal law and spirituality are intertwined with the land, the people and creation, and this forms their culture and sovereignty. The health of land and water is central to their culture. Land is their mother, but it also demands their responsibility to care for it.

Tom Dystra, an Aboriginal elder, says:

"We cultivated our land, but in a way different from the white man. We endeavour to live with the land; they live off it."

On one notable occasion the relationship between our family and our indigenous brothers became a little strained. Dad was working in the west, recovering from the financial collapse of his crushing plant. Usually, he would finish work around three o'clock in the afternoon on a Friday and drive six or seven hours home, arriving around eleven o'clock. He stayed until ten pm on Sunday and then drove back to the job and worked for another couple of weeks, after which the scenario would be repeated. This went on for years.

One night when I was about fourteen years old, Dad arrived home on Friday night and found a dozen or so local aborigines having a noisy party at a campfire they'd set up about twenty metres from our house. Most of the local indigenous population lived on Brown's Flat in Nowra, and corroborees or get-togethers on top of a hill formed part of their ancient culture. We lived on Brown's Hill. This night they sat close together, singing, laughing and shouting in a full-on party, awash with liberal amounts of alcohol, constant noise and the sound of breaking bottles.

"How long this going on for?" Dad asked.

"They've been coming here on weekends for some time now and the noise goes on through the night," Mum replied.

Dad was not willing to call the police in case of reprisals, especially when he was away in the west during the week. In an earlier incident when Julie was only six months old, an aboriginal woman had run into our place to escape her violent husband. The woman's partner threw rocks, which smashed the window above Julie's cot and splintered glass over the blankets. Luckily, Julie wasn't in the cot at the time. We lived without close neighbours. We had no second car, and with Dad away most of the time, we were vulnerable. Also, Mum didn't have a car licence.

The night grew longer and the noise louder, so Dad and I stole quietly into the garage and went to his cache of explosives, preserved from the days of the crushing plant. I knew where he kept them, but I never touched them. Having seen what they could do, they commanded my greatest respect. Dad took two detonators, two fuses and one stick of gelignite, and we crept around the side of the house, over the fence and, taking a wide arc, crawled to the far side of the partygoers. At a safe distance from the mob, Dad broke off a quarter of the stick of gelignite and connected the fuse to the detonator, then repeated the same procedure with the remaining three-quarters of the gelignite. While the yahooing continued, Dad lit the fuses, and we retraced our path silently to the fence.

An unexpected explosion from a random detonator can give you more than a fright at fifty paces. Combine this with exploding gelignite on a still night in the bush and it could easily be taken as a sign of the dawn of Armageddon. The quarter charge went off first, as planned. A blue and yellow flame streaked across the surface of the bush, and the explosion shook the ground. Everybody froze and went silent, their bodies silhouetted against the flickering fire.

We aimed to get their attention with the first charge, and we achieved that successfully. Everyone stared, open-eyed, at one another. Nobody moved until the second explosion. I'd experienced the sound of exploding gelignite inserted in drilled holes in Dad's quarry, but the noise is reduced when it's contained in rock. I'd never experienced an explosion on the surface of the ground. The second explosion was deafening—louder than anything I've ever experienced. Blue and yellow light flashed, providing a mysterious, sinister backlight to the ghostly gums. The ground shook, and the roar from the three-quarter charge made its statement. Terror overtook the mob and, miraculously sober now, they scattered instantly in every direction and disappeared. No more parties bothered us after that: problem solved. Explosives were a friend and helped us in many ways.

* * *

Dad's long struggle with life continued, but one day a chance meeting renewed his strength. It also planted a seed that grew during my youth. Dad needed parts for his loader and drove from Nowra to a supplier in Sydney. At the counter of the business, he struck up a conversation with another customer. The guy had a familiar accent.

"You sound like you're a Latvian," Dad said.

It turned out that he knew Dad's godmother, who lived in Ohio in America. This was the first news he'd received about any friend or family member since he'd arrived in Australia. Dad returned from Sydney with a broad smile and announced the exciting news. He wrote to his godmother and learned that his mother, his brother John and cousins were alive in Riga. Dad's face shone and lit up the lounge room when he told us. It was a rare moment to see Dad so full of emotion. For years he'd hidden his grief about the likely death of his mother and family. I was so happy for him.

Because of that contact, Dad commenced writing to my Uncle John in Latvia. Communist authorities read all incoming and outgoing mail, so letter writing needed great care. Dad asked if his brother needed anything, and Uncle John replied with 'boots' or 'shoes'. So Dad sent them regularly. Dad became determined to return to Latvia, and he spent hours dreaming up ways to sneak into his beloved country.

Whenever Mum became suspicious that he was secretly plotting a return, she'd say, "Arnold, don't even think about going back. It's too dangerous, and we may never see you again. Is that what you want?"

Mum's heart went out to Dad. She understood even more than I could imagine the pain he carried being wrenched from his homeland. She carried the wound of the ridicule and failure of his business, and she feared that one day the longing to reunite with his mother and brother, to walk through the fields of his farm and stroll the streets of his beautiful Riga would be overwhelming. He would go and, like others, not return. While the news of my grandmother and uncle were greeted with great joy, it also produced a strange tension. Dad's concern was his mother, aged well beyond her years by the severe climate and hardship of Siberia. Time was running out if he wanted to see her again.

Invisible tension became a constant presence in our home, only becoming apparent when Mum discerned that Dad was secretly dreaming. Her anxious pleas continued to torpedo his hopes of a return. Unknowingly, I absorbed that tension and held it inside. I could not put words to it. That came later.

My relationship with Dad grew more distant during my adolescent years. He needed to pursue work away from home to repay his debts and keep food on the table. His absence contributed to the tension between us. Weekends were the only time he came home, and often, when working on a project in the far west of the state, he vanished for weeks. I loved the early days when we worked side by side in the quarry. But now, Dad withdrew into himself. The cruel blow of the failed business took its toll. I struggled to understand him and longed for his companionship. I craved his acceptance, but never heard him say, "Well done", or give any other hint of encouragement.

One day when I was twelve years old, Dad and I were driving back from the crushing plant at Milton, South of Nowra, when he told me how he respected me for my work on the plant. I've never forgotten that moment. I can still see the section of road in my mind when he caressed me with those beautiful words — they were like gold. *I did mean something to him!* The following six years, until I turned eighteen, he spent away from home, working on earth-moving contracts around NSW, trying to recover from the financial disaster that ended the crushing business.

My relationship with him in adolescence often felt awkward. He was not open to giving or receiving a hug, and communicating was difficult because of his lack of English and heavy accent. I struggled to understand him and was embarrassed to invite mates around because they also found it hard to comprehend what he was saying.

* * *

My saviour was sport. My athletic prowess at cricket and rugby league not only gave me inner strength and confidence, it also provided opportunities to broaden my experience and learn survival skills that would help me survive my later adventures.

My skill at throwing a football and cricket ball developed in childhood through the questionable practice of stone throwing. In my teens, we spent much time playing in the bush, throwing rocks and spears at just about anything. One of our groups' favourite activities was a good rock fight. You won when you drew first blood on your opponent. It was all high adrenalin stuff. To get hit with a rock, hurt. Fast reflexes were required to duck and weave, and then let loose with your throw, hopefully with deadly accuracy. I developed the skill of throwing a flat rock so it curved around a tree to hit my opponent. Of course, these blokes were my mates. Can you imagine what it may have been like if we were enemies?

Somehow we survived those days without loss of life and limb. I had a good arm as a cricket player. Early in the senior ranks, I entered a throwing competition during one of the knockout competitions. It cost twenty cents, and all the hopefuls threw their twenty cent coin into a cricket cap. My mates urged me to have a go, and I stood there for a minute looking at the cricket cap filled with twenty cent pieces thinking, *I can't afford it.* I earned only fifty cents a week pocket money, so I decided not to enter. While I believed I could throw, I didn't think I could win. However, my mates wouldn't hear of me not having a go and pressured me until I finally relented. I broke the record of 276 feet by throwing 336 feet, which still stands today. Once, I threw the ball from under the goalpost at one end of the field in Nowra Showground through the goalposts at the other end of the field and took the prize money. I loved throwing and could throw as hard as I liked without hurting myself. I realised after years of boyhood battles in the bush that the body is like a sling. I could co-ordinate my wrist, elbow, and hip—my whole body—in perfect timing to propel an object.

In November 1976, I entered a football-throwing contest in Berry along with thirty-six other contestants. Three throws were permitted, and after two rounds the contest lay between a local basketball player, Dennis Marshall, and me. Marshall's final throw appeared to land on the same mark as mine. An engineer's special tape was produced, and I was awarded the title by nine centimetres with a throw of forty-six metres and thirty-nine centimetres. Sadly, the Guinness Book of Records could not register my achievement because of a technicality.

When I was a junior, Dad took me to sport, but that ended when the great debt from the crushing plant debacle hit him. Approval from him was part of what I wanted to achieve from immersing myself in cricket and rugby league, but he was never one to give praise. It was the Latvian way. He told me I could always do better, and I think that spurred me on, but it came at a cost to our relationship.

One unforgettable day in the history of my sporting career came in my early teens when I was average at cricket and rugby league and struggled to make the team. I had an average batting score of around twenty-two for the season, and though our team had never scored more than 200 runs, we did reach the grand final in C Grade against Berry. On the first day Berry opened with a score well over 300. The following day I walked to the crease as opening bat, feeling intimidated by the odds stacked against us. I glanced up and discovered Dad sitting beside Mum on the side line. He'd not been to a game for many years, and I was dumbstruck. Energy rose in my body. I was so proud to have him there. All my senses suddenly sprang to life. I watched the ball leave the hands of every bowler. Nothing was going to stop me. I ended up scoring a century and we won the grand final. The only time I scored a century. What a difference a Dad makes! He didn't say anything after the match but his presence was powerful.

As I look back, I realise how much sport shaped my character. It not only gave me fitness and physical skills, but the ability to be a team player. While we practised planned moves in league[2], the real test was to quickly assess the situation, respond appropriately and remain calm under pressure. I believe it helped me develop resilience, determination, self-reliance and to take calculated risks—essential skills for a young bloke thinking of hitchhiking around the world and sneaking into Russia to find his family.

One final event in developing survival skills in the 'school of hard knocks' occurred when I played league for Berry and received an elbow in the throat. At halftime, I couldn't get air into my lungs. I was gasping and in distress, and I soon found myself in Shoalhaven Hospital with attentive staff watching over me. A young doctor told me I needed a tracheotomy, but because of his lack of experience he would not perform it. That meant an hour's travel by ambulance to Wollongong Hospital. The cost of the ambulance was $360, and I'd just recently cancelled my medical cover because of the pressure of mounting expenses. My current wage as a junior engineer netted me only thirty dollars a week, so I told the doctor I was happy to drive myself to Wollongong Hospital.

He just stared at me and said quietly, "The ambulance will be here in a couple of minutes."

He was right. When it arrived soon after, two paramedics quickly transferred me to the back of the wagon and attached an intravenous drip. With a nurse by my side, we left for Wollongong hospital. Through the back window, I saw an ambulance wagon following.

Then a voice from the radio in the front of my wagon said, "Car one to ambulance three. Don't you have a critical patient on board?"

"Yes."

"Well get your lights and siren going and get a move on."

The wagon instantly leapt forward, lights flashing and siren screaming. Thus began a hair-raising ride to Wollongong. Fortunately, I knew the road well and prepared myself for the notorious bends at Kiama. I braced myself. We screamed around those bends, and I was thrown from side to side, hanging on desperately to the stretcher because they hadn't strapped me in. I feared the needle from the drip would be ripped from my arm, and I imagined what the pain might be like and what mess it would make. The last bend was skilfully negotiated, and I momentarily relaxed, exhausted, perspiration running down the back of my neck. I had to suffer in silence as the injury had robbed me not only of air but also voice.

After a trip I'll never forget on that early Sunday evening, I landed safely, but wasted, at Wollongong Hospital. The ambos rolled me straight into intensive care. The nurses removed my football gear and adorned me in hospital garb. The medical staff watched me closely during the night and the following day. Tuesday morning I woke from a good sleep, the swelling had gone down and I looked and felt human again. And I was hungry, very hungry. No, I was starving. Usually, I didn't eat before a match, and that meant I hadn't eaten since Sunday lunch. I heard the breakfast trolley rattling along the corridor and, as I prepared for a welcome breakfast, I happened to turn around and notice a sign above my bed that said, 'Nil by Mouth'. I quickly stepped out of bed, turned the sign around and slipped back under the sheets. Almost instantly a pleasant lady in a hospital uniform walked into my room with a menu.

"Oh, you can eat?" she said.

"Yes," I whispered confidently. "I don't have much voice, but I'm breathing much better now."

"That's good." She handed me the menu.

I looked over the meals on offer—weetbix, muesli, cornflakes or porridge; eggs poached or fried or scrambled; sausage, fried tomato and bacon; toast with Vegemite or honey—and I ordered everything on the menu.

"My, you *are* hungry," she said with concern.

I arranged myself in bed, ready for my feast. Twenty minutes later, she returned with a tray heaped with food. Every mouthful was delicious.

I was eying the sausage when suddenly the sister burst around the curtains and exclaimed,

"What are you doing? Who turned that sign around?" She called for my breakfast angel and ordered the food to be taken away.

"This man could have an operation any minute. He's not supposed to eat anything." Her command put a dramatic and abrupt end to my meal.

An hour later, the doctor appeared at my bedside. I composed myself, and while I couldn't speak clearly, tried to convince him I was well enough to be discharged from hospital. He nodded and, after carefully considering my charts and looking me over again, he gave the all clear for me to go home, but only on the condition I had a family member drive me or go by ambulance.

Since I no longer had hospital cover, a family member was the only alternative. My brother and father were both working, and I understood they couldn't help. So I went to reception dressed in my scruffy football gear (nobody had come to see me) and lied in the best voice I could manage.

"My brother is coming to pick me up in an hour's time."

Paperwork completed, I took the lift to the ground floor, quietly slipped out the front door, then walked down the street and hitchhiked home. Fortunately, I received a lift to Nowra, but asked my kind driver to drop me at Kiama. The few mouthfuls of food I managed to steal at breakfast had not even touched the sides. I had a few coins in my pocket, so I bought a dollar's worth of hot chips and managed to hitch a ride home to Nowra. I don't think I ever told my parents the full story. I learned later that Mum had paid the ambulance insurance!

Chapter Four - Exploring My Limits

"Only when there are things a man will not do
is he capable of doing great things."
Mencius

Another occasion that caused me grief on the footy field occurred later in my career. I'd played as a NSW Country representative as well as for the Southern Division, and on two occasions I'd been selected for the team against sides from Great Britain and New Zealand. I'd decided it would be my last season of football. During the first half of a match at Nowra showground, I received a solid knee to my face while trying to tackle their winger. I didn't think too much about it, being the first tackle of the game. I played to half time, but as I walked off the field, I touched the side of my face and couldn't feel anything. I finally left the game twenty minutes before full time when our team was well in front and in no danger of losing. The medic diagnosed it as a depressed cheekbone. Two weeks later, I underwent surgery in Port Kembla Hospital. The local newspaper wrote, 'Jirgens may not play again', but I did.

During the New Zealand match, we faced giants in black and white, including one of the biggest men I've ever seen. This Maori stood six feet eight inches, eighteen stone with cut-away sleeves revealing arms thicker than my thighs. Though I was the biggest in our team, this giant dwarfed me. To make matters worse, I didn't want to be there. It was a cold winter's day, the ground was like concrete and I was lacking motivation. The referee warned he would send off anyone who threw a punch.

We packed down for the first scrum, and I locked in against the Maori mountain man. My job was to take the ball up to the opposing team, and his job would be to take me out. Feeling scared, I avoided eye contact with him. Then I noticed that one of my teammates, a meathead with the reputation of being a street fighter, was firing up. Coach regarded him as a loose cannon, unpredictable at the best of times, but I predicted what was about to happen, and it did.

Meathead started punching one of the New Zealand front-rowers. A brawl was about to break out. I had a split-second to decide. Do I take mountain man out or do I let him floor me? I sprang forward and grabbed him in a headlock just as the brawl exploded. He screamed out to me to let him go, but that would have resulted in my instant death. I gripped tighter while he threw punches, but due to my deadly grip, they didn't land with any venom. Mountain man didn't have a neck. Somehow his shoulders, covered with a mass of muscle, tapered to his head. While I grimly held on to his head, he flung me around like a rag doll, lifting my feet off the ground. Finally, the brawl finished, and his testosterone subsided. I let go, and mountain man settled. It was one of the scariest moments of my life. I had no idea at the time, but the rough and tumble on the football field, the necessity to think and act quickly, the fitness and endurance, would contribute to my survival overseas.

Exploring my limits and facing my fears got an extra boost when, during my nervous induction into the workplace, I rebuilt my first car, a Vanguard with a Massey Ferguson tractor engine. I was the only student in Nowra High who owned a car, thanks to a reasonably-sized paper run I worked at fifteen. After six months

I'd saved fifty dollars, and when I mentioned it to Dad, he said, "You need to buy a car."

"You can't buy a car for fifty dollars."

"Yes, you can." He went out looking and came back a week later with the news that he'd found something suitable in a bloke's backyard. It'd sat there for four years corroding in the weather.

"How much does he want for it?" I asked.

"Fifty dollars."

We towed it home. It had sat in Sam Ray's yard for so long that kikuyu grass grew up through the bonnet. The motor had been reconditioned, but the elements had overtaken the body — it was a rust-bucket. The following twelve months I persevered on restoring it to working condition. I was sixteen and loved the challenge of resurrecting this old beast. None of the electrics worked, so I rewired it with 100 feet of yellow cable. I renewed the indicators, an illuminated arm which rose from a slot in the door pillars. I found eight litres of green paint in the boot, so scrubbed down the body to remove the rust and gave it a new coat of paint. I upholstered the seats, painted the dashboard, and twelve months later, just before my seventeenth birthday, my beautiful fifty-dollar Vanguard with a reconditioned Massey Ferguson tractor engine was ready for the road. It was a great day when I drove my labour of love out of the garage and down the street. I had always travelled on a pushbike, so having a car was a huge step up.

My mechanical innocence resulted in dramas. I understood nothing about fuses when I rewired the car, and one day while driving with a mate, smoke suddenly appeared from under the dashboard, followed by flames.

"Look out, we're on fire," my mate screamed.

He opened the door and prepared to jump out, but leaping from a car when it's travelling at thirty-five kilometres an hour is not recommended. I grabbed him with my left hand and stamped on the brake pedal. The car stopped and the fire went out. I sat for a few minutes, then started the engine and drove on without incident, the acrid fumes the only reminder of our brush with danger.

Another memorable event occurred when I began work at the council. My boss asked me to take construction plans to a worksite. During the journey, I noticed a strange odour. *What's that?* I wondered. Suddenly, flames shot out from under the dashboard. My first concern was for the plans. I reached up under the dash and wrenched the wires free. They were hot — very hot — and the wire's melted plastic coating wrapped itself around my fingers. I screamed. Flesh and wire became one, my skin badly burnt and blistered. It took weeks for my fingers to heal. For the first week I couldn't close my hand. I drove one-handed for the next two weeks.

My car proved a stepping stone to greater things. Dad's truck, though a solid unit, was old. The handbrake shook itself to pieces, so Dad removed it and kept it in the garage until registration was due the following year. A skilful driver, he could easily manage the truck without a handbrake. When I began driving it, I had to be on the alert for the engine stalling. If the engine cut out, the brakes wouldn't work because they needed air pressure provided from the motor. It wasn't a good idea to stall the truck on a slope or any precarious place. The other problem was that the starter motor didn't work, so we could only clutch-start it. That, of course, meant that whenever the engine was switched off, the truck had to be parked in gear on an incline!

An early test of my driving skills came with the atomic power site project at Jervis Bay. Dad allowed me to help out on the 'cut and fill' job that required tipping the load of topsoil down a hundred foot embankment.

The dogman, who is a kind of safety supervisor, said, "Hang the back wheels of the bogey over the edge of the embankment."

If we did this, the load would fall easily to the bottom of the slope, but the tricky manoeuvre was a challenge. My mind went blank for an instant, and I took huge breaths to remain calm. The edge of the embankment was soft. I had no handbrake—control required the manipulation of the clutch, the accelerator and fifteen gears. It was a lot to think about at once. I was seventeen years old, unlicensed, and had one foot on the accelerator and the brake simultaneously. My other foot rested on the clutch and rolled back gently to allow the back wheels to drop over the edge of the bank. The next challenge was to time the lift to release the load, knowing that if I stall, the truck and I were gone. Gradually, I rolled the truck back, thinking, *I can't ever let my foot off the accelerator.* The back dropped, so I depressed the clutch to raise the hoist and threw it into forward gear, keeping the accelerator depressed. Perspiration dripped from my chin in the hot cabin, and my heart raced, but I completed the manoeuver.

This, one of the scariest moments of my youth, gave me valuable experience. After repeating it many times, I believed I could handle just about any vehicle on the road.

The real break came when the other drivers working on the site noticed my skill in handling Dad's truck. I could use the gears to control the speed rather than the brakes and managed not to over-rev the engine. The men were working a six-day week and keen to have a break at the weekend, so they offered me the opportunity to drive their trucks on Saturdays. I earned $15 a day and thought that was big money because I only got fifty cents pocket money a week. As a bonus, I could listen to Frank Hyde, the rugby league commentator, on Saturday afternoons and enjoy the football. Listening to the radio while I drove the latest model air-conditioned Mercedes trucks felt like being in heaven. My car kept me broke, and I always looked for ways to earn extra dollars.

I played basketball with mates on Monday nights, so I offered to pick them up for five cents—that helped. Then I hit on a great deal. Dad had a contract to transport five hundred tonnes of material from a subdivision in Cambewarra to Nowra. Soon after he received the contract, he wanted to visit a friend out west and said I could do the job on his behalf. He offered me a dollar a load.

"He can't do it. He hasn't got a truck licence," Mum said, glaring at my dad with her hands on her hips.

Dad shrugged. "He'll be okay."

I was keen to give it a go, not only for the money's sake but also the experience. It required me handling an eight-tonne loader to fill the twenty-tonne truck, the largest truck in Nowra at the time. To turn the bogey vehicle it took seven turns of the steering wheel, lock to lock with no power steering. When I came to a ninety-degree bend with it fully laden, I had to get up from the seat to gain extra strength to turn the wheel. The first day on the job I did nineteen loads, and on the second, eleven. By the end of each day I felt as if I'd spent three or four hours working out in a gym.

Chapter Five - Altitude Training

"Let me not pray to be sheltered from dangers,
but to be fearless in facing them.
Let me not beg for the stilling of my pain, but
for the heart to conquer it."
Rabindranath Tagore,
Collected Poems and Plays of Rabindranath Tagore

Entering the workforce provided further terror-inspiring opportunities to prepare me for the challenges of risky overseas exploits. The ability to stay relaxed while balancing on a beam at a dizzying height above the ground became an unexpected advantage during my future travels.

I completed my last exam for the HSC on a Friday. The day after I finished, I walked across the road from home to a business owned by the father of a friend from school and asked if he could give me a job.

"Yeah, sure I can. You can start Monday," he said with a smile.

Wally was a steel manufacturer and built large sheds for farmers and businesses in the area. On Monday, I enthusiastically bounded out of bed and turned up for work at the job site at Integral Energy. A series of posts stood in the ground, loosely bolted, waiting for a crane to lower huge trusses into position on top of the posts. Someone had to climb on top of a steel column, ten metres off the ground, and guide the trusses into position so they'd line up with the holes in the posts, and then bolt them into position. I didn't know at the time, but the workman who'd been doing that job had fallen and gone to hospital the previous Friday morning with two badly broken legs. I'd turned up in the afternoon and landed his job. So up on top of the column I went.

The RSJs were massive. An RSJ is a steel beam in the shape of the letter H lying on its side. The task needed one workman to stand at one end while I stood at the other end and guided the heavy beam into position. It then required walking along the RSJ to secure it to the top of the posts. My companion on the other end confidently walked along it to the posts, but there was no way in the world I could repeat his performance. I stared at the ground, ten metres below and thought that it didn't look soft to land on — even five metres would have been unacceptable. If I fell, I was dead. There was no way I could walk on the top section like my colleague managed effortlessly. Nervously, I straddled the RSJ and walked along the lower section. That meant my calves rubbed along the upper edge of the beam. It worked, but I was not as fast as my experienced colleague, and my anxiety sky-rocketed when I had to turn around on the beam and return to my starting point. By morning tea, I'd removed the skin off my inner calf muscles where they constantly rubbed against the top of the beam. During this break, my new workmates told me that the guy whose job I had, fell the previous Friday. It didn't help!

That was my introduction to the workplace. After I survived the entry-level test, I then had to move to the next level, many metres higher. The following day I presented myself with chafed thighs to the paper mill at Bomaderry where Wally had a contract for maintenance work. The water tank sits there to this day and is around 100 feet above the ground with a ladder attached to the side of the tower. The rusted bolts on the top third of the ladder needed replacement. This required me to climb to the top section with a huge drill, manoeuvre outside the cage enclosure around the ladder and drill and replace the bolts. Up I went. The climb inside the cage was easy, but by the time I reached the top section, perspiration drenched me and I breathed heavily from the weight of the drill. The cars travelling along Bolong Road appeared the size of matchboxes. I tied a rope around my waist and secured it to the cage, then started on the first bolt. I drilled and drilled, and the bit jammed regularly. The days working on that tower were the longest days of my life, but Wally seemed pleased with my efforts, and the experience stood me in good stead for the future.

* * *

As the years passed, my interest in Latvia increased. It became a magnet that often drew me away from the task at hand. But even if was safe for me to travel to Dad's homeland, I still needed to undertake considerable preparation, and money was the first requirement.

I went for an interview at the council. It was located in a large room in the council chambers. A photo of the Queen, and photos of past shire presidents lined the walls. Around the large wooden table sat twelve men, intent on listening to my every word and watching every move I made. The shire clerk was present, the shire president, the water and sewerage engineer and nine councillors. Three of the councillors were men who were part of the group who contributed to Dad's near bankruptcy. I was very anxious and reminded myself to relax and breathe deeply.

"Are you afraid of heights?" the engineer asked.

"No." I desperately wanted this cadet engineer position, so I wasn't going to say 'yes' to any question like that in an interview.

I survived the interview, and the shire clerk asked me to turn up the following day for work. They gave me three months' probation so I had to perform, otherwise I would lose the position and plenty of others waited in the wings.

The next day the chief engineer drove me out to the site at the seaside town of Huskisson. "I don't ask any of my men to do anything that I'm not prepared to do myself," he said as he drove.

I wondered, uneasily, what he had in store for me, but my respect for him grew enormously during the day as I remembered that comment.

We stopped at a huge reservoir perched about twenty metres above the ground on four concrete columns. It held 50,000 gallons of water. What task would he give me? I couldn't back down. My temporary status meant he could sack me, no questions asked.

A cage ran from ground level up the side of the reservoir to the top. That sight triggered a memory. I recalled the construction of the reservoir behind our home when I was fifteen. It was smaller and not as high as the one in front of me, which stood twenty-five metres high. I'd been fascinated by the construction and watched its progress every day. A bald-headed bloke in a white shirt and tie had often climbed around it, and his daring had amazed me. I looked at the engineer standing beside me at the foot of the Husky Reservoir and realized that he was that guy—my new boss, Ian Ross.

"Peter, do you think you can climb to the top and walk around the other side?" Ian asked.

"Sure, Mr Ross."

So, despite my racing heart, I scrambled up the ladder under the safety of the cage, but when I reached the top there was nothing to save me from falling. He wanted me to walk around to the other side, no handrails, nothing to hold onto. I thought if I fall from here, I'm gone. If I slip, I need to make sure I fall into the water. So I started out, arms outstretched either side to help keep balance, and, gingerly, step-by-step, I made my way nervously around to the other side. Ian Ross stood looking up.

"I'm here, Mr Ross," I called down when I arrived.

"Okay, now look down," he called up to me, "and you'll see

a valve. Can you tell me whether it's open or closed?"

"Open," I replied.

"Thanks. You can come back down now."

But I froze. I could not turn around. I lowered myself until I knelt, then tried again, but I still couldn't turn. It would've been better if I'd continued to walk all the way around, but I didn't realise it then. In desperation, I jumped around and almost over-balanced. Again I froze. Then I began to tremble and thought, *I'm not going to make it back without falling.* I stood there for a couple of minutes, unable to move, talking to myself. *Settle down and relax. You can do it. If you can't, they'll get rid of you.* I took a deep breath, steeled myself, then slowly shuffled back around the edge and climbed down the ladder.

"What happened up there, Peter?" Ian asked. "Did you freeze?"

"Yes, Mr Ross."

He grinned. "Never mind, it's good character building."

Next stop, the Barrier Pumping Station about thirty metres above the bank of the Shoalhaven River. Inside are massive 800 horsepower pumps and huge shafts that drop down to the river. A tunnel allows water to enter an enormous cavern from which the powerful pumps suck water up to the reservoirs.

"Peter, I want you to climb down and crawl along the tunnel into the cavern. I'll be inside the pumping station, and I'll ask you a question."

I nodded, then descended into the tunnel and found myself in knee-deep water. It was pitch-black, so I found my way along by touching the cold walls, my hands searching the rough sur-face to find the way ahead. Next minute, bang; my head hit an object — the pump head, sitting about 200 millimetres from the floor of the cavern. "Mr Ross, I'm here now."

"Can you tell me how much sand is in there?"

I stooped down and calculated. "There's about 100 millimetres of sand on the floor."

"Okay, thanks, Peter. You can come out now."

I understood the process. The pump head draws the water through the pipes into the reservoir above and is set above the floor to avoid sucking up sand. The sand has to be regularly removed because in times of flooding, sand builds up and is drawn into the pumps, which wears the impellers. They usually do this by backwashing and blasting the sand back out into the river. Having successfully completed the task, I turned around and groped for the tunnel entrance. Around the cabin I went, once, twice and then a third time, but I couldn't find the tunnel. *Am I going crazy?* I thought.

"Peter, you can come out," Ian called.

I began to panic. While groping around in the darkness for the entrance, I continually banged into the pump head and the pipes connected to it. For ten minutes, I searched and struggled in the darkness to find the entrance. Finally, I found it. My body relaxed with relief. I'd kept missing the opening because I'd been feeling around at shoulder height and the tunnel was much lower. On my way back, near the entranceway to the pit, I hit my head on a sharp rock and felt blood running down my face. Eventually, I emerged, happy but bruised and bloodied, and we were soon back in the car. The cut bled for some time, but fortunately it was on my left temple, so Ian, sitting in the driver's seat, couldn't see the handkerchief pressed to my head. I'd thought that if he saw my injury, he'd think I was incompetent and would sack me. How crazy was that!

That was my first day at work. I realised afterwards that he'd been testing me. Soon after my initiation, Ian suggested it would be good experience for me to spend a month at the Nowra sewage treatment works.

"Make sure you take your lunch down," he told me.

I thought he must be joking. He wasn't.

Being the labourer, I received all the crap jobs, sorting out the solids and other unmentionable tasks. No way could I eat down there. Everyone else who worked there didn't seem to find it a problem, but I couldn't manage it, at least not for the first three days and then I got used to the smell. I spent four weeks immersed in that foul environment, after which I expected to go to the office wearing my nice new shirt and tie.

However, Ian said to me, "Go and dig trenches for four weeks. It'll be good for you."

So off I went to dig sewerage and water main extensions. In total, I spent the first six months in the field, involved in all the council's manual jobs. Looking back, I see it was valuable experience, probably the best thing that could have happened for my career. It gave me an understanding of a wide range of jobs and work environments, and the opportunity to work beside a variety of people. I liked Ian Ross and respected him. He was encouraging, supportive and thoroughly professional. I learned later that some of the council staff who'd prevented Dad from getting council work because he was a 'wog' had pressured Ian not to hire me, but Ian Ross was a fair man and judged a person on their merits. Maybe that was why he gave me such a scary and challenging workout to qualify for the position.

In later years, he confided in me, saying, "You were the best person for the position. The thing that clinched it for me was your car. I was impressed that a young bloke at seventeen owned and renovated a car."

I never admitted that the council plans he gave me to transport to an office came close to going up in flames in that car.

My ability to survive entry into the workforce left me with the belief that I could endure just about anything. I wanted to expand my wings and see the world, but that required money!

Chapter Six - The Ache Develops

"Never was anything achieved without danger."
Niccolo Machiavelli

One evening when Dad was going through some of his old papers, I spotted a document where the Australian government had stamped the authority for his entry with a DP number.

"What does DP stand for?" I asked.

Dad, surprisingly, was keen to speak. He settled back into his old chair, and what followed was a rare moment of meeting of minds. The rain beat against the windows of the lounge room, and I had to strain to hear the words that for Dad were full of emotion and meaning. I had to listen carefully to catch his words, even though I was used to his accent.

"We known as DPs or displaced persons. Some say about eleven million people became refugees in Europe at end World War II — amazing mix of nationalities. About seven million were forced or voluntary labourers. They brought to Germany by Nazis, prisoners of war, political prisoners and Jewish survivors of concentration camps. Included soldiers forced into German military from occupied territories - people who fled their homes because of war or political reasons. They scattered through German territory and placed in camps. Latvian refugees among them."

I listened, wide eyed, stunned to hear of the size of the refugee population.

Dad continued. "So big refugee problem—so Allies first create Supreme Headquarters Allied Expeditionary Force to decide who are refugees. It distinguish between people outside their countries and had to be repatriated or resettled, and people who still within borders of their states. Only people still within borders of their states ... ah ... classify as refugees. People who were outside their countries and needed to resettle were called displaced persons or DPs. Overnight we became a number. We then were DPs, not people anymore. The Americans and British militaries were responsible for DPs until United Nations Relief and Rehabilitation Association (UNRRA) could take over."

"Dad, that is so humiliating," I interjected. "Prisoners of War were known by their number."

Dad said nothing in response to my outburst. He paused and continued.

"Allies created UNRRA during World War II to help out regions liberated from Nazis. First job—repatriate refugees soon as possible. Between May and September 1945, UNRRA sent home around six million people, and due to Yalta repatriation agreements between the USSR, the US and Britain signed in 1945, they force many of the DPs who fled from Soviet Union to return. That decision resulted in great distress and suffering for many refugees."

"How could they do that?" I asked in amazement.

"Well, I guess it considered best decision then. Very difficult to get countries to agree at best of times. And that's not the end of story. I'll come to that in a minute."

Dad closed his eyes for a moment, then continued, "The Soviets declared all DPs were war criminals, Nazi collaborators, spies, adventurers, people who sabotage ..."

"Saboteurs," I offered.

" ... saboteurs, traitors ... common criminals, and demand their immediate repatriation. Also, Soviet government insisted DPs were Soviet citizens, because according to Soviet laws, without government's permission, no individual who no longer want to be belong to their country…

"Renounce their citizenship," I helped.

"Yes, Soviets said people could not do that. Not end them being Soviet citizen. Soviet repatriation campaign was brutal. Soviets pressured political refugees to go back — but they refuse to return. Some did, but other refugees later found out they were sent to Siberia as criminals or conscripted into the Russian Army where they die. When refugees learned none of the people who had gone back — Latvians had not reached Latvia, their fears were stronger — they became more determined not to return." I could clearly understand now Mum's fear about Dad's longing to return to Latvia. The Soviets were still in charge, nothing had changed.

The emotion in Dad's voice revealed the sadness that sat below the surface. He usually kept his thoughts to himself, and it was particularly rare for him to speak so openly about this chapter of his life. Sadness mixed with anger gripped my chest. I could only imagine what it had been like for Dad and the millions of others who were wrenched from their roots and thrown to the wind.

Dad continued, "UNRRA caught in difficult position. On one hand — had to resolve refugee problem quickly as possible and resettle them somewhere. On other hand, Soviets pressured UNRRA to force refugees to repatriate. Any discussions about resettlement got negativity from Soviets. UNRRA not want to displease Soviets, but refugees refuse to go — so sympathy of Western governments toward them got stronger. At same time, many UNRRA member countries, including the US, continued to have strict immigration controls — not allow large numbers of European refugees. Also, corruption and everyone not working well together was big problem in UNRRA. It was a waste of time and money."

"How did America and Australia come into the picture?"

"Well, UNRRA's repatriation mission fail for Latvian refugees — they refuse to go back to Soviet-occupied Latvia. In long run, British and American authorities decide to ... reinterpret their early agreement with USSR and agree to repatriate only individuals who claim Soviet citizenship. The rest — treated as DPs. This allow US to support the Balts who refuse to accept Soviet citizenship, because their country was forcefully incorporate into USSR. This made USSR angry and then Baltic refugees became big source of tension between Soviet Union, United States and Great Britain. Then, in February 1946, United Nations Assembly pass a resolution and allow people who had valid objections to being return to USSR not be repatriated. This decision very good — stop repatriation campaign."

"What happened next?"

"Problem then — what to do with remaining DPs. In the middle of going on ... I mean ongoing conflict with USSR, USA and Britain about Baltic refugees — in 1946, United Nations set up International Refugee Organisation, IRO. Soviets strongly oppose formation — try many ways to slow down IRO's work. IRO pressure some countries to think again their restrictions and accept DPs. It successful with Australia and Canada — but US remained closed." Dad let out a long sigh.

"Though it's tough in Australia, we are safe — have food on table and roof over our heads."

My heart felt heavy for Dad. He was uprooted from his homeland, became a number in the system and arrived in Australia only to be treated like a second-class citizen. I wanted to help him. If only I could make him feel better.

An ache developed during these rare openings of the windows of Dad's mind. The need for acceptance from my father was part of what first stirred the desire for my main mission. I also longed to see the land of my roots and thirsted for adventure. During the days of my youth, this developed into a compulsion with an intensity and urgency that even today I don't fully understand. It seemed to grow not so much from my mind, but from an energy, which refused restraint, surging from the depths of my being. My longing to leave the Shoalhaven, which I'd outgrown, and my home country, which now seemed too small, grew every year. I was ready to conquer the world.

My relationship with Dad hit its lowest point when I was twenty-four, just before I began my Latvian pilgrimage. I lived at home because of my engineering studies at Wollongong TAFE, and I often arrived home at eleven o'clock exhausted from working and studying. I couldn't afford to live away from home and was grateful that Mum and Dad were keen to support me. However, I felt cornered, trapped, and I longed to hear words of affirmation from Dad.

During this time, I gained a reputation as a sportsman. My success in rugby league resulted in my photo and story appearing on the front page of the *South Coast Register*. People I didn't know congratulated me on the street, yet when I came home, my father didn't say a word; nothing but silence. I ached for his acceptance, even a hint of congratulation. It never came, and I grew angry. When I raised the issue with him, he said, "If I said 'you did well', you'd relax and never do your best again."

I couldn't understand him believing that myth. I pushed him and he pushed back. Our relationship became physical, so I decided to move out of home.

* * *

In 1979, at the age of twenty-six, the yearning to visit my family overtook me, and I decided to risk visiting Latvia. I felt I had to go to my father's birthplace, to take the journey he could not do and find his mother and family. It was a dangerous hope. Since Dad was still classified as a Soviet national, I too, as his son, also could be called up into the Russian army if I set foot on Soviet soil. Despite this threat, I began preparations for my mission. It would take me into the heart of the Soviet Union, and expose me to situations that were far from safe. I also longed for adventure. Canada, the USA, Scandinavia and the beauty of Europe called me. The Shoalhaven had been my playground, my preparation, but now I was ready to explore beyond, poised to visit places I had read and dreamed about.

My brother John, who was travelling in Europe at the time, had tried to visit Dad's mother and brother. He'd paid to travel from Stockholm to Leningrad by ship, hoping to catch a train to Riga, but he hadn't been allowed to board in Stockholm. No explanation was given and no refund for his ticket. John does not give up easily, and he'd hitchhiked to Helsinki and tried again, only to be refused once more. After further enquires, John booked a 'Culture Tour' from London, which included two days in Moscow and two days in Riga. He'd managed to sneak away from the tour in Riga for a brief time and had contacted Dad's family. He'd taken a big risk, but he'd managed without the authorities being aware of his movements, and a brief visit was better than no visit at all. Now I wanted to take up the challenge.

After much soul-searching and conversations with family and friends, I made an application to the Soviet Embassy in Canberra to visit Latvia. Of course I could not reveal my real purpose — to find my grandmother and family. That would put my family and me at great risk.

Twice the embassy phoned and asked, "Mr Jirgens, why do you want to visit Riga?"

"I've heard it's a very nice city to visit," I replied. "I've read a lot about it, and it sounds very interesting."

"That's very unusual," came the reply.

I had to earn extra money and fast, so I signed up at Woolworths for three hours, three mornings a week as a cleaner. In six months, I raised raise enough money for my tour. I could get six months' leave without pay from the council, and with annual leave included, it gave me seven months for my trip. The only way I could enter Latvia was through Moscow, and that required travelling with a registered tour operator. The only foreigners who could travel unaccompanied in Soviet Bloc countries were businesspeople and diplomats. I booked a tour and was set to go. With seven months' leave, I decided to see as much of the world as possible first. It would also look good on my passport to have Canada, America and the UK as part of my travel itinerary. An exclusive nine-day trip to Soviet states may have aroused more than curiosity.

Chapter Seven - Mission Launched

"I learned this, at least, by my experiment: that if one advances confidently in the direction of his dreams, and endeavours to live the life which he has imagined, he will meet with a success unexpected in common hours."
Henry David Thoreau, Walden; Or Life in the Woods

1980 was an eventful year: the thirteenth Winter Olympics were held at Lake Placid; nuclear tests were fashionable — the French on Muruora Atoll, with the United States, the Soviets and Britain all joining the radioactive chorus; Mt Helens blew its top in Washington State; the United States and other countries boycotted the Moscow Olympics because of the Soviet invasion of Afghanistan; *The Empire Strikes Back* premiered; John and Yoko posed nude; Reagan defeated Carter in a landslide; and the twenty-seven-year-old son of a hardworking Latvian immigrant boarded an aircraft in Sydney and flew to Canada.

I understood that I could get a cheap, one-hundred-dollar flight from Montreal to London, so I flew to Vancouver — a beautiful city that sits majestically on the seaside of British Columbia — and hitchhiked across Canada. Many said that Vancouver was one of the best cities in the world in which to live, and I loved it, finding it clean, safe, and attractive, flanked by picturesque ocean and mountains. After my long flight, I enjoyed walking around the park that runs out into the sea.

One afternoon after I returned to my accommodation, I noticed one of the local football teams having a training session on an oval across from the Youth Hostel. They belonged to a Canadian gridiron league, which is similar to the American game. I stood watching awhile until one of the players—a man about my height, heavily built, square-faced with a crew cut—walked over and asked if I played football.

When I told him that I played rugby league in Australia, he introduced me to the team members and invited me to have a run with them. My new friend, the quarterback, explained the rules of the game and offered to show me how to throw the football. The football they use is much smaller than the ball we use in rugby league and much easier to throw. I could torpedo throw a league ball a fair distance but to throw a gridiron ball was magic. We spent an hour going through the different drills and moves, and then we threw the ball back to each other, which I think prompted him to say, "If you want to be a quarterback in American football, this is how far you need to throw the ball."

The ball flew from his hand around thirty metres and sailed over my head and bounced a couple of metres behind me. I picked it up, threw it as hard as I could and watched the ball soar over his head, landing well beyond where he stood. Apparently, that was the worst thing I could have done. He wouldn't speak to me, just wandered off with the rest of the team while I stood there by myself. I guess he thought I was a smart-alec and deserved it for showing off.

After my brief taste of gridiron, I finished absorbing the sights and sounds of Vancouver, then hitchhiked through the Rocky Mountains, making my way east. The snow-capped peaks made our mountains look like molehills. Cool, crisp air touched my lips and filled my lungs, making me feel high. A guy whose occupation was catching rattlesnakes picked me up in the Rockies, and I stayed at his place for three days. He had permission from the local Indian tribe to search for snakes and milk their venom, which he sold.

"Would you like to come along for the ride?" he asked.

My first reaction was dread. Snakes and I don't mix, but then I thought, *why not?* I climbed into the cab beside him, and a short time later, we stopped at the reservation.

He spotted the first of the well-camouflaged snakes within minutes of getting out of his truck, and caught three or four in the first hour. This daredevil, who seemed to have X-ray vision, took my breath away with his daring. We moved to a steep, dry ravine and descended among large rocky outcrops. I readied myself to jump onto a rock a metre below, but as I crouched to leap, a split-second before take-off, I noticed that a rattlesnake lay curled up on my landing point. It was too late to back off, so I did my best to launch myself further into the air and landed roughly three metres below the sleeping serpent. I spun around as the snake raised its head and rattled its tail—a sinister sound. The snake handler, using his left hand, pinned the snake's head to the ground with a forked pole. His right hand gripped its body behind the head and then began milking the venom into a smaller container he carried on his belt. For the next two hours we crawled over rock ledges on our hands and knees because of the steepness of the gully. The slippery rocks were the same colour as our prey, and I nervously followed the master snake-handler, my heart pounding with every movement. Every time he stopped I remained frozen, while, in a flash, his weather-beaten hand seized the tail and repeated the milking process. By the end of our excursion I was exhausted, physically and emotionally.

A few days earlier, I'd picked asparagus beside the road—a less dangerous exploit—and I'd stored at least two kilograms in my backpack. In return for my snake-handler's generosity, I gave him the asparagus, which his wife served for dinner that evening. I can't remember what else we ate, but I know it wasn't snake pie!

A few days later, a generous Canadian couple on their honeymoon gave me a lift in a utility. "If you don't mind riding in the back, you're welcome," the friendly bloke said.

"Thanks, you're very kind. That's fine."

The only space they could provide was the floor in the tray behind the cabin. It gave me an uninterrupted view of the stunning countryside, but though it was spring, snow and ice still covered sections of the countryside, and it was freezing. I survived by clothing myself in thermals and crawling into my sleeping bag. Lake Louise remained frozen, and a black bear casually wandered along the edge of the forest. My heart sang for joy at the magic moment.

At that time, disaster hit Canada. Mt St Helens had erupted, spewing a column of gas and ash twenty-four kilometres into the atmosphere. The fall-out covered hundreds of kilometres, killing fifty-seven people and thousands of animals. The heavy grey cloud of ash hung over the picturesque countryside. It remained for three days.

Though the incentive of a cheap airfare to London had taken me to Canada, connecting with my father's cousins gave me another reason to visit. One lived in Sudbury, a large city in Ontario with a humid continental climate of hot summers and long cold winters. The town had once been a large timber centre and a world leader in nickel mining. Thomas Edison visited Sudbury as a prospector in 1901 and is credited with the discovery of a large ore deposit in the region.

My visit to the Steinbacks, Dad's cousin, his wife and their son, a professional motorcyclist, marked an important milestone in my quest. Not only because they gave me the address of my grandmother in Riga, but also because I thought Dad would be thrilled to know that I'd made contact. It was a relief to finally arrive at their two-storey, weatherboard and shingle-roofed house, typical of American and Canadian homes. They answered my knock on their door with smiles and open arms, and I basked in their warm welcome. I loved chatting with them about Dad and the family, and I felt as though I knew them through Dad's stories from their time in Latvia.

I stayed in Sudbury for a few days, travelling into the centre of the city and wandering the streets to catch the flavour of the place. One day, the lively sounds of banjos and fiddles drew me to a park where a blue-grass festival was in full swing. I stretched out on the soft grass to enjoy the free concert, and at the conclusion, I introduced myself to the slightly built guitarist.

"Hi. I loved your music. Where are you from?"

"Latvia. The whole group are Latvians."

When I told him that I too was Latvian, he turned to the group, who were packing their instruments away. "Hey, guys. This fellow is Latvian."

They all grinned and nodded, and after they finished packing, we spent time chatting about their tour and my trip. How remarkable to meet Latvians in the middle of Canada!

Dad's other cousin lived at Niagara Falls, so that was my next scheduled stop, and after time on the road I was keen to rest for a few days at their house in the suburbs. Their welcome was as warm as the Steinbeck's, and they gave me the royal treatment. Family photos, beautiful food and stories from Latvia overwhelmed me. I also visited their son Karlis, a professor of English, and met his family.

I saw the distinctive features of Dad in his uncles, in their faces, eyes and, of course, large hands. It was special to connect with these people on the other side of the world, my family, my flesh and blood. I am so grateful for their kindness.

* * *

I crossed the border into the US at Niagara Falls and soon found my place beside a friendly driver. Some hours later, he said, "I'll be turning off the main road in about ten miles. Where do you want me to drop you?"

Despite the remote area, I was not too concerned because I had a tent and sleeping bag, but I only waited for ten minutes before a guy about my age stopped and invited me on board.

"Where are you from?" he inquired — the usual question that opens up conversation between a driver and a hitchhiker. He found out I was an Australian and said, "I want you to join me and my mates and have a party."

What a party — what a night! I love spontaneity. Just when you think you'll be alone in a remote region in a foreign country, surprise! Experiences like this enticed me back to the US later when I hitchhiked for five months. I found the Americans to be hospitable people, and I enjoyed my time there.

I checked my dates and discovered that I had time in my schedule to venture north, through New Hampshire, Maine and New Brunswick, before flying to London. While my main mission was Latvia, I also wanted to experience as much as possible of other cultures. Travel is an education, and I wanted to grasp it with both hands. Every detour, every encounter, enriches.

I arrived at the Bay of Fundy on the Atlantic Coast, near Moncton, on a sunny day with a gentle breeze. The images I'd seen and the action of the tides I'd read about drew me to this place like steel to a magnet. The bay stretches over 270 kilometres wide and has huge tides. Each day, 100,000,000,000 tonnes of seawater flow in and out of the bay. During one tide cycle, more water is displaced than the combined flow of the world's freshwater rivers. The funnel-shaped bay contributes to the power of the surge. Here I witnessed the highest tides in the world.

I stood on the edge of the river when the tide was out and the riverbed exposed, scanning the bay, when at the distant edge of the bare expanse of sand, I heard and saw a wave approaching at speed, announcing the turning of the tide. Close to a metre high, it moved at a pace which could have overtaken an experienced marathon runner. It was breathtaking, standing alone, experiencing this eerie natural phenomenon. I decided to camp on the shore and explore. I eyed a sign that stated the times of the tides each day. Was I brave or stupid enough to race the tide?

The next day, I decided I'd risk it. I left the edge of the bay and walked quickly with the outgoing tide almost to a group of islands about one kilometre from shore. My gaze fixed on the water's edge, keeping alert for the first sign of the return of the sea. I kept a respectful distance from the edge of the retreating water to ensure I had a healthy start for the race to shore. Eventually, the water stalled for a moment and the wave began to form. I'd decided to run from the moment it turned, and I headed back, thinking I'd judged it well. Minutes later, looking back over my shoulder, I saw the wave gathering speed, so I quickened my pace. I felt as if I were back on the football field running with the ball, only on soft wet sand rather than a hard grassy surface.

The wave slowly gained on me, and I put every drop of energy into the last 300 metres. My heart pounded and my legs screamed from lactic acid, but I enjoyed the race. My football fitness helped me reach the shore just ahead of the wave, then, standing breathless on the safety of a rock, I watched the huge surge of water wash past me up the river. Soon the powerful incoming current restored the river to a respectable height in readiness for a repeat retreat to the sea hours later. I loved it—I was alive!

Back on the road again, I met a band and travelled with them for three days, going to their gigs and partying until five in the morning. We slept in till noon and then drove on to the next place and did it all again. Decadent!

Nova Scotia and its capital Halifax unfolded before me. Well-groomed farmlands, windswept lighthouses, historic villages and rugged coastlines took my breath away. On a street in Halifax, I asked a guy for directions.

"Where are you from?" he asked.

"I'm an Aussie."

"Do you play rugby?"

"Yes, I play rugby league in Australia."

"I belong to a local club in Halifax. Would you like to train with the team tonight?"

So I turned up and discovered that out of the four local teams, one would be selected to tour Newfoundland for three weeks with all expenses paid by a wealthy benefactor. I think I was the only player who didn't drop the ball during training, and they invited me to join the team. It was a great compliment, but not possible due to time restraints. Sadly, I had to let this opportunity pass. What adventures might have developed from that detour?

As the main purpose for my trip crept closer, some days I wondered if I'd allocated too much time to wander the countryside. The urge to find my grandmother and uncle sometimes overtook the joy of the present. Such moments only happened occasionally, usually waiting for a lift in uninteresting countryside; however, the dates had been set, and I could not alter flights and tour times. The intoxication of constantly changing sights, sounds, and smells soon removed any frustration or impatience. Around every corner lay the unexpected with a challenge I needed to respond to. I'm grateful for the freedom of my Shoalhaven playground, for the experiences at work and Dad's quarry that provided me with confidence, independence, and the thirst for adventure, insatiable.

* * *

When my time in Canada finished, I flew from Montreal to London and spent a month hitchhiking through the UK, including the green-carpeted countryside of Wales. One day in central Wales, I came to an enormous roundabout, a hundred metres in diameter with five exits leading out to all points of the compass.

I struggled across the busy roads with a fifteen-kilo backpack swaying behind, dodging cars and trucks until I found the road to continue my journey. I walked one hundred metres before a car pulled up and a middle-aged couple asked where I was going. I told them I was heading for a youth hostel in a town one hundred miles or so from the roundabout.

"We live this side of that town," the driver's wife said.

I thought they might take me as far as their place, and I could then hitch the final distance to the town, but her next sentence surprised me.

"But we don't pick up hitchhikers, do we, Harold?"

"No, darling," came his obedient reply.

I understood. Many drivers were anxious about picking up hitchhikers. After all, I could be an axe murderer!

"Where are you from?" the woman continued.

"Australia."

"Australia! Does your mother know you're hitchhiking?"

"I think so—eh, I'm not sure. I don't think I told her."

The woman's eyes widened, seemingly shocked. "You should consider travelling by bus."

I stood for at least five minutes beside her car while she expressed her concern and advised me to let my mother know I was hitchhiking. The traffic continued to swish past as I politely and patiently waited for her to finish her mothering. It finally came, but before I could respond, she said, "You probably could stay at our place for the night."

"Oh, that would be nice," I replied quickly.

"But we don't pick up hitchhikers. What food do you eat? Do you eat steak?"

I stood beside the car feeling that my chances of hospitality with this cautious Welsh couple hung delicately in the balance. "Sure, I do," I said with a smile. It must have been the right answer or her maternal instincts were so highly activated that she accepted it; she gave me the okay to join her and Harold.

I accepted the invitation and climbed into their car. A little later, Harold stopped the car at their terraced house in a little town of a couple of hundred people. Their place was one of ten, neat double-storey terraces clustered together in the middle of town. Harold worked in the mines and had some interesting stories to tell about his underground exploits. His wife, Gwenfa, continued her mothering.

"Are you cleaning your teeth twice a day?"

I assured her I was taking good care of myself, and the evidence I displayed from my slim, suntanned body confirmed it.

"I'd like to write to your mother. Can I have her address, please?" she said in a way I couldn't refuse.

When I returned home from my trip, my mother read me the letter Gwenfa had sent the day after my stay with her and Harold. She wrote how she and her husband had picked me up hitchhiking, and that I was cleaning my teeth and appeared healthy so there was no need to worry. For thirty-three years until my mother's death, they continued to correspond with each other. Mum had a great collection of Welsh tea-towels displayed in every room. I imagine Gwenfa had a similar collection with pictures of koalas and kangaroos. Mum also sent photographs of the family and cut-outs from the newspaper when I had success in sporting activities. Every time I visited Mum, she would give me an update on Gwenfa's family, Harold's health or the latest happening in town. They were wonderful people. A beautifully cooked meal and the warmth of their welcome added a touch of home to my travels.

Mighty castles stand majestically through north and mid-Wales. Castles, swords, armour and stories of King Arthur had filled my imagination as a child, and now, here I was, immersed in this land of boyhood fantasy. I'd not seen anything like these castles before. Built during the medieval period, Beaumaris,

Caernarfon, Conwy and Harlech are landmarks in the development of medieval military architecture, now recognised as World Heritage Sites. The great fortress-palace of Caernarfon, with its soaring walls and imperious towers, is perhaps the most famous of the four. Yet all are equally inspiring. Harlech, spectacularly perched on a crag, overlooks sea and mountain. Gritty Conwy, surrounded by a ring of amazingly well-preserved town walls, produces a convincing medieval atmosphere. Beaumaris, in pure architectural terms, is the most accomplished medieval fortress in Britain. These awesome stone fortresses built by the English monarch Edward I to stamp his authority on Wales don't stand alone. The landscape is dotted with castles of all kinds. Medieval conflict moulded the history of north and mid-Wales. The Isle of Anglesey bears widespread evidence of prehistoric settlement in the shape of mysterious burial chambers. I drank it all in.

I stumbled on the Great Orme, a prominent limestone headland on the north coast of Wales, next to the town of Llandudno. After my trip, I learnt that the ancient copper mines discovered below the Great Orme dated back over 4,000 years to the Bronze Age. Archaeologists fully uncovered the mines in 1987 when they discovered a large underground complex thought to be the largest known prehistoric mine in the world. They believe the mines were abandoned around 600 BC until the Romans reopened them. They were utilised at various times during the Romano-British period.

One of the most interesting features of Wales was the myths and legends you meet at every turn of the road. Everywhere you go in Wales, someone will point out a hill, church, a standing stone, lake or castle which has a story of its own. My favourite, the tale of Prince Llywelyn, came from the village of Beddgelert in the National Park of Snowdonia. The village of Beddgelert (Gelert's grave) owes its name to this site.

Chapter Eight - "Don't Go"

"In all of us there is a hunger, marrow deep, to know our heritage — to know who we are and where we came from. Without this enriching knowledge, there is a hollow yearning. No matter what our attainments in life, there is still a vacuum, emptiness, and the most disquieting loneliness."
Alex Haley

The warm welcome of friends made my arrival in London easy. This was to be a pivotal point in my journey. In Australia, I'd written to the Foreign Affairs Department and mentioned that my father had been an Australian resident for the last thirty-five years and was still a Soviet citizen — Dad had always said that he was born Latvian, raised Latvian and would die Latvian. I, however, was an Australian citizen, and I enquired if his status posed any problems for me visiting Latvia. I heard nothing and assumed all was well for my visit.

After three weeks in the UK and less than twenty-four hours before my flight to Moscow, where I would begin the guided tour I'd paid for in Australia, I rang Mum from my friend's flat in London. She sounded relieved to hear my voice, but when I said I was flying into Moscow tomorrow, her response was, "Peter, we don't want you to go. We've just received a letter from the Foreign Affairs Department, and they advise that because your father was not naturalised by 1965, he is still deemed a Soviet citizen. If a Soviet national has a child outside the Soviet Union, that child is still recognised as a Soviet citizen. You could be conscripted into the Soviet Army as soon as you arrive in Moscow. We don't want you to go, and if you do go, you go at your own risk."

The Minster of Foreign Affairs, Andrew Peacock, had signed the letter.

I was shocked to hear this news; devastated that the Australian government had officially warned me not to go, and distressed because both Mum and Dad no longer supported me. I imagined what Dad would say if he learnt I'd been forced into the Russian army. "We told him! What was he trying to prove?"

I wanted Dad to respect me, but this certainly wasn't going to help my cause. Shattered, I sat there not knowing what to do. I'd worked and saved so hard. The plane would leave Heathrow Airport at one p.m. the next day. That night was agonisingly long. I wrestled with the pros and cons for hours. Could I risk it? Should I cancel my trip and abandon my mission? I finally fell into a fitful sleep.

The next morning, I awoke and peered out the window to see the sun shining. *Not bad for an English summer,* I thought. But the English sun didn't penetrate the dark clouds that filled my mind. I dragged my feet from the bedroom to the lounge room and sat down for breakfast with my friends.

"I can't go," I announced sadly. "I won't go. It's stupid, especially when I don't have the backing of the government. If I get into strife, they won't help me. My parents are against me going. They'll be very upset if I risk it."

My friends remained silent and nodded, but I read the shock on their faces. They understood how much this trip meant to me. It was not a sightseeing tour. It was a mission that had taken hold of me at the deepest level. The words left my lips, providing a brief moment of relief, but then the longing returned, stronger than ever. At ten o'clock, two hours later, the pendulum swung the other way and remained firmly in place. I changed my mind. If I didn't go now, I'd never go. I was prepared to suffer the consequences, whatever they were. I farewelled my friends, boarded the plane and flew to Moscow.

* * *

The threat of a severe electrical storm hung in the atmosphere as my aircraft approached Moscow airport. The plane hit an air pocket and dropped out of control. Passengers screamed and grabbed the armrests. It seemed to go on forever, but it was probably only around twenty seconds before the aircraft resumed its course. Heavy breathing helped my recovery, but other passengers, wide-eyed, continued to grip the armrests of their seats. I looked over Moscow, shrouded in sinister grey, and a chill ran up my spine. The next half-hour would be my first real test. Would my journey finish here? Would I be sent back to Australia? Would I be seized by the Soviets and forced into the army? My anxiety grew by the minute.

The plane taxied to a halt some distance from the terminal. The rain had ceased but the tarmac was wet. Two buses drove out to meet the aircraft to transport passengers to the arrival hall. Then, to my horror, an army jeep containing six soldiers, four with submachine guns, pulled up at the bottom of the gangway. Two of the soldiers quickly positioned themselves at the foot of the stairs. I froze in my seat at the front of the aircraft. Passengers collected their belongings and pushed past me, but I couldn't move, convinced the soldiers had come to get me.

You idiot! You'll never see your family again. This is it. The Russian army will conscript you.

At that point, I seriously regretted my decision to take the trip and resolved not to leave the plane. If those guys wanted me, they would have to come and get me. I wasn't prepared to walk straight into their hands. I wouldn't go easily.

Every other passenger left the plane, and three concerned stewardesses came to see what my problem was.

"What is the matter, sir?" they asked in broken English. "All the passengers have left the plane. Everybody is waiting for you. The buses are waiting for you. What is the problem?"

I felt it futile to try to explain the situation to them. They wouldn't understand, so I just sat there, not moving.

Many times they repeated, with growing frustration, "What is the problem, sir? What is the problem?"

Perspiration ran down the back of my neck. Sitting in the safety of Australia months ago, deciding to enter Russia had seemed easy. But now, facing the reality of Soviet soldiers and the threat of military service, I can't believe I made such a stupid choice. The stewardesses became frantic, at their wits' end, so I nervously picked up my hand luggage and turned to the open door.

I glanced down the gangway at the two soldiers standing either side of the stairs on the tarmac, and they glared up at me. My heart raced, and I froze again. The two buses, engines running and crammed with passengers, sat waiting. I wanted to retreat into the aircraft, but it was too late. It took me forever to descend the dozen stairs to the tarmac. I kept my head down, and when I stepped onto the tarmac, I fixed my gaze on the nearest bus, avoiding eye contact with the two soldiers. I stepped between them, barely breathing, waiting for them to grab me from either side, waiting for the sharp, authoritative, "Stop! Show us your papers." I didn't hesitate, just kept walking towards the bus. It didn't seem real. But no order came to stop. No physical restraint occurred. I stepped onto the bus not believing that I'd made it. I took a deep breath and my body relaxed—until the thought came that they might be waiting to arrest me inside the terminal, then my anxiety returned. I wasn't safe yet.

The bus pulled up at the terminal, and I walked into the reception hall. Airport staff directed everyone on the aircraft, except me and another guy, in one direction—apparently they were on their way to China—and ushered me and my fellow traveller towards another part of the terminal. We stood for a moment in the massive terminal, empty of passengers. At least one hundred guards, dressed in khaki uniforms, stood around the perimeter of the huge hall. I presumed they were army personnel but later discovered that all government employees wore this military style uniform. I felt exposed, vulnerable, and walked anxiously to the counter, where an unsmiling officer stood straight and rigid. I produced my passport, disguising my fear as best as I could. All sensation from the waist down left my body, leaving me completely numb. You can't imagine my relief when the officer stamped my passport, handed it back and gestured me through to baggage collection. I made it!

My luggage and I were soon reunited, and I left the empty terminal and easily found the taxi from the airport to my accommodation that was included in the guided tour. During our drive through the quiet streets of Moscow, the taxi driver asked me where I was from. When I told him, he said, "Australians good, U.S. bad. We like Australians because you come to the Olympic Games."

His comment eased my fear a little, and other Russians echoed his sentiments later.

Cars were few and the pedestrians many in Moscow. Thousands of souls wandered along the footpaths in a colourless, homogeneous mass—same shoes, same clothes, same umbrellas. I arrived at my hotel, a large complex built for the exclusive use of tourists, and from my window on the tenth floor, drank in the breathtaking view of Red Square and St Basil's Cathedral. I found the varied beauty of the architecture and the magical atmosphere stunning. I couldn't believe that the Square, now centre stage for formal military parades that display the might and power of the Soviet armed forces, had once been a slum housing peddlers, criminals and drunks.

The next morning I faced a dilemma. If the tourists in my tour group got to know me, I might have problems when the tour reached Riga, where I needed to sneak off and find my grandmother. They would most likely ask what I was doing, and that could lead to serious problems for me. So I decided to steal away from the group before they formally assembled for the day tour of Moscow. Of course, that made me vulnerable. The authorities could arrest me simply because an approved Russian tour guide or official always had to accompany foreigners. Nevertheless, I decided to risk it. I strode out of the hotel door, thinking I could hide in the masses. Three days wandering around Moscow might be boring, but I reminded myself of the real purpose of my tour: to find my grandmother and family. That had to take priority. I'd paid five hundred dollars for the tour, which included Moscow, Riga and Leningrad, and I believed it was good value since it enabled me to meet my family. It was a means to an end. I'd made a meagre nine dollars an hour as a cleaner, so it'd been a great effort to make this trip happen. However, I believed the investment was worth it. Meeting my family didn't have a price attached to it. I would do almost anything to contact them, to represent my father, to share his heart with his family and then return to Australia, conveying their love and affection to Dad. This was what drove me on.

Chapter Nine – An Unscheduled Meeting

"Home is a notion that only nations of the homeless fully appreciate and only the uprooted comprehend."
Wallace Stegner, Angle of Repose

Having survived entry into Russia without any real incident, I assumed I could stay trouble free. Thousands crowded the streets of Moscow. I could hide in the masses; I'd be safe. But I discovered, in my two remaining days in the city, that was not to be the case. Red Square, just outside the hotel, remains, as it has been for centuries, the heart and soul of Russia. Few places in the world bear the weight of history as Moscow's Central Square does. From St Basil's Cathedral, one of the most famous pieces of architecture in the world, to the great pyramid of Lenin's Mausoleum, Red Square is rich in symbols of Russia's turbulent and intriguing past. Moscow overwhelmed me — the place, the space, the grandeur and the history. Where would I start? I lit a cigarette and strolled to the centre of the Square. Almost immediately, an athletic-looking, round-faced Russian, about my age, approached me and asked something. I said I didn't speak Russian.

He nodded, his glasses glinting in the sunlight. "Are you English?"

"Yes," I replied cautiously.

He smiled. "Could you give me a light?"

I produced my lighter and lit his cigarette. He told me he was a schoolteacher who lived in the town of Perm, 1500 kilometres away. His wife was also a schoolteacher, and they didn't have children. He taught English in the local school, but I was the first English person he'd met. He was rapt. I was stunned, curious and cautious. We walked together and continued talking about anything and everything. I became desperate to sit down, but he wanted to keep walking.

He seemed intelligent and inquisitive, but rather uptight. I suspected he might be anxious talking to a Westerner, but most Muscovites walked with an air of unease. Though I walked reasonably relaxed beside him, I felt as if a sinister, unseen force filled the air. I didn't realise it at the time, but he was continually checking to see if we were being followed. The reason why became frighteningly clear to me the following day.

During this remarkable encounter he revealed what it was like to live in a communist state. People's access to housing in Russia was similar to their access to consumer goods; it depended on their position in society and their place of work. Most families lived in a single room in a communal apartment, where they suffered from overcrowding and had little hope of improving their situation. Dress was an instrument of propaganda, strictly regulated like everything else. It had to be planned and approved. Clothing had to conform to the requirements of 'good taste', being 'clean cut', 'easy and economical to produce'. The Soviet authorities labelled boring clothing as 'never going out of fashion' and promoted it as 'eternally youthful'. Also, clothing was intended to have a disciplinary influence, so it would develop 'right attitudes' and 'good behaviour'.

I learnt my Russian friend came to Moscow two or three times a year to buy food for his family. Even though Perm was a large city, people had to line up at five o'clock in the morning at the dairy factory to buy milk. Many items of food were scarce. He came to Moscow to buy cheeses and dried meats that were not available in Perm. In Moscow he usually met with his grandmother, aunt and uncle. We continued walking for the rest of the day, deep in conversation, my new friend, unknown to me, continually checking if we were under the scrutiny of the secret police.

As the afternoon wore on, he asked if I would like to go to his aunt's place for dinner. I was more than happy to meet his aunt, uncle and grandmother, and it would give me respite from endlessly walking the crowded streets. I needed somewhere to sit for a while. Later, I learnt that walking helped to hide from security. Standing and talking was one of the quickest ways to catch the eye of the secret police.

He phoned his aunt, and she said I was welcome. I wanted to take a gift for my hosts, and I found a shop, ten metres wide and forty metres long, that sold nothing but vodka. There must have been fifty brands of vodka in bottles of all shapes and sizes and varying quality. Five dollars US provided me with two bottles of top quality liquor. I'd brought three hundred US dollars from Australia, knowing there was a black market, which would improve my travel fund. I planned to give the money to my family in Riga.

We climbed to the tenth floor of an apartment block — a carbon copy of most of the apartments in Moscow, prefabricated, modular and colourless — and entered his aunt's apartment. He introduced me to his extended family, who were preparing dinner. The flat was basic and bare — everything a boring beige. I sat down with my new friend — what a relief to take the weight off my feet! A program on the television caught our attention.

Russian generals in full uniform, helmets on, were sitting around a table addressing about fifty schoolchildren in their midteens. Planes appeared on the screen, followed by trains, cars coming out of factories, power lines and telephones.

"What are they saying?" I asked my friend.

"The generals are saying the children must work hard for

the mother country because their parents have worked hard and were clever people who invented planes, cars, trains, electricity and the telephone."

"I didn't know Russia invented all these things," I said cautiously, thinking this man was a schoolteacher who wouldn't believe such nonsense.

"Oh, yes," he replied. "It's in our encyclopedias."

I frowned. "I thought someone else invented the telephone."

"No, let me show you." He reached for a large book written in Russian and opened it to a page. "See, here it is."

Of course, I had no idea what the writing said, but the power of communist propaganda stunned me. I was aware of how much effort Russia had invested in the Olympic Games. They had over two thousand sport institutes, and if a child or young person showed any athletic ability, they were removed from their family and immersed in rigorous training. The family had no say in the matter. East Germany and Russia produced many gold Olympic medals that year and used their triumph as part of their propaganda assault on the west.

The simple meal of potato and meat stew was most welcome. During dinner, grandmother said, "We have vodka", and out came one of the bottles I'd bought. The bottle was opened and someone had the first drink, then grandmother sculled her glass. "Vodka good," she said.

I hadn't realized until then that Russian culture demanded sculling, not sipping. The bottle moved clockwise, and I was next in line. With all eyes on me, I poured a nip and threw it down. It tasted like petrol and burnt every inch of the way to my intestines. Tears I couldn't stop ran down my cheeks. I was so embarrassed.

"Vodka good?" Grandmother said, looking at me.

"Yeah, vodka good," I lied.

The bottle kept circulating the table until it was empty, at which point I was greatly relieved. Apparently, tradition requires that when a bottle is opened, it has to be emptied. The meal continued, but a short while later, grandmother demanded, "More vodka."

I almost choked on a mouthful. My heart sank. More vodka! More petrol. More pain. What were they thinking? The second bottle was opened and sculled in the same manner. I regretted my generosity in providing two containers of torture, but at least my charity hadn't extended to three bottles. As I was leaving, my kind hosts insisted on giving me two coloured wooden spoons. They were probably the most valuable items they had in their home, and I was embarrassed at their insistence that I should take them. I tried to refuse, but my friend, their nephew, advised me to accept them; it would be an insult if I refused. I left with a full stomach, a scalded esophagus, wonderful Russian friends, and two wooden spoons, which sit on my study shelf to this day.

I walked back into the foyer of my hotel on a high. What a day! Then came the low. It was as though I'd been in another world, and I was not prepared for what happened next. Although, as I look back, I should have been. I confidently strolled up to the desk to collect my key.

"Where have you been?" demanded the woman behind the counter.

My anxiety rose instantly. I didn't know what to say.

"Where have you been?" she repeated in a more menacing tone.

I was speechless for a moment, then I stuttered that I didn't understand, trying to put her off.

She had none of it. "Where have you been?" she screeched.

"What's the problem?" I asked with as much innocence as I could muster.

"It's after dark. You don't go out after dark unless you are going to the concert or the ballet and you get tickets from here. Where have you been?" she shouted again.

Everyone in the foyer stopped and looked at me. *I don't need this,* I thought. *Here I am trying to keep out of the spotlight, and suddenly I'm on centre stage. This could go badly for me.* I couldn't find words. My mind went blank. She continued to scream at me. In desperation, I finally blurted out the first thought that came into my mind, "I couldn't sleep and had to go for a walk."

"That is not good," she replied harshly. "You must not go out after dark, only to the concert or ballet, and you must get tickets from here."

I nodded, trying to look contrite.

She gave me my key, and I quickly retreated to the stairs and took refuge in my room. Another close call, but somehow I managed to survive. I put my head on the pillow and within minutes fell into a restless sleep.

Chapter Ten - Are We Being Followed?

"In the West, people watch TV.
In Soviet Russia, TV watches you."
Comedian Yakov Smirnoff

My visit to Russia occurred during the Brezhnev period. As it had been in previous decades, the KGB was considered the world's most efficient information collection agency. Their slogan, also adopted by the Stasi in East Germany, was 'Our motto is to know everything'. Comedian Yakov Smirnoff's famous joke said it all: 'In the West, people watch TV. In Soviet Russia, TV watches you.' Espionage was a deadly serious game. Suspicions and tensions ran high. All foreigners residing in Russia and the Soviet Bloc were strictly segregated in walled and guarded compounds, drove specially marked cars, and shopped in hard currency stores. Russian citizens could not freely mix with foreigners and could not enter tourist hotels. To this day I cannot explain how I managed to successfully avoid detection.

On my second day in Moscow, I left my hotel early to hide again in the masses on the street. Nobody had questioned me about my absence from the tour group the previous day, and I was willing to risk it again. I chose not to have breakfast that morning because at least half of the tour group were in the dining room. Buoyed by my accomplishments of yesterday, I returned to Red

Square and thought I would explore the city. The day was warm, and already pedestrians crammed the footpaths. I wandered around Red Square, and after about thirty minutes, a slim, sharp-featured man approached me. His dark hair was receding on top, and I thought him probably in his late thirties.

"Do you speak English?" he asked.

How does he know that? Why did he pick me out? I wondered. *Could he be a* KGB *agent?* Feeling uneasy, I said nothing.

Speaking in English, he offered me a free, guided tour of his city so he could talk and practice his English. I told him I was on holiday and accepted his offer. However, I engaged my radar. I had to be careful.

"Where do you want to go?" he asked.

"Take me to all the places where tourists don't go."

"Okay, you follow me."

So we set off to explore the road less travelled in Moscow.

A little later, he asked, "Do you have any American currency?"

"Yes," I replied hesitantly.

"It's ten to one for the US dollar on the black market," he said with a grin.

My eyes widened in surprise. I'd received only one for one yesterday on the official exchange at the bank.

"I can increase your money on the black market," he added, his eyes sparkling.

It sounded like a great offer, so I gave him twenty US dollars. Within seconds, he disappeared into the teeming mass which covered the footpath. I waited and waited and became anxious. Would he return? Have I done my money? I waited for fifteen minutes and still no sign of him. I'd just resigned myself to having been duped for twenty dollars when suddenly he appeared and handed me two hundred roubles. I was blown away. He'd just given me more than a Soviet doctor would earn in a month (180 roubles). *This guy is for real,* I thought. *I think I can trust him.*

However, I had no intention of revealing the true nature of my visit to Moscow and the Soviet Union.

As we walked, he talked about the evils of the Soviet system and their insidious propaganda. He described communism as nothing more than a form of slavery, a religion without a god, an ideology in which the government *is* god. That's why the abolition of religion, nationality and private property are communism's primary objectives. The Polish poet Aleksander Wat, who committed suicide in 1967, was racked with guilt over the part he played as a perpetrator, one who had made the intellectual world safe for Stalinism. A passage from his autobiography records:

> 'The loss of freedom, tyranny, abuse, hunger would all have been easier to bear if not for the compulsion to call them freedom, justice, the good of the people.'

My new friend's knowledge was extensive, and he spoke with passion. The Soviets had used their Olympic gold medal tally to boast how superior and well-fed the Russian people were. However, they didn't make public the fact they had around 2000 special institutes where they trained young people from an early age who had the potential to be good athletes. The Soviets took my talented cousin in Riga from his parents when he was twelve years old and placed him in an institute of music because of his musical ability. While my uncle and aunt had no say in the State's decision, they were happy, because it gave him the opportunity to further his education and develop his musical talents.

Victor, my new friend, reminded me about the rules of taking photographs in Moscow and any communist controlled territory. No soldiers, no military equipment, no military installations, no pictures of the grey lifeless concrete slabs that thousands of Muscovites called home. No photos of the long queues of starving peasants and workers who waited patiently for whatever they could buy from the limited stores they were permitted to access. I broke all the rules about taking photographs, mastering the sneaky shot wherever I could. I was keen to include military personnel, especially in Red Square, and invited one of the locals to take a photo of me with soldiers in the background. Victor was insistent on changing the angle to avoid capturing them but I kept encouraging him until he finally relented. Fortunately, the soldiers were not aware of what was happening. Occasionally, I decided to join the queue outside a store only to find shelves almost bare of food items. Inside, I managed to take a few secret photos under the cover of my coat. How desperate these people were for food and the basics.

My relationship with Victor grew quickly, but I also became increasingly cautious, presuming he may want me to pass an opinion on the politics of the Soviet system. Was this guy trying to snare me? He was so open about the dark side of communism. The communists had earlier jailed him for twelve months, simply on suspicion of talking with a US journalist. They had no hard evidence, but in this State suspicion was all that was required to lock people away. He didn't tell me where he worked, but he obviously had some security and an income. He told me that he'd recently completed a book.

He led me down some stairs into a seedy underground bar. The air, layered with the stench of beer, fish, tobacco smoke and human odour, hung thick and unmoving. You could have cut it with a knife and served it on a plate. Patrons, mostly noisy men, crammed together in small bunches, laughing and talking in words I didn't understand. My friend wrestled in his pocket for some kopeck and walked to the side wall, which resembled a urinal. He inserted the equivalent of about twenty cents US into a slot, held a glass directly below a spout protruding from the wall and pressed one of a series of buttons. Beer flowed into the glass. When full, he handed it to me. Sprats and herrings were available to complement the beer. I thought it a weird place.

We sat down at an old wooden table with our beers, and I asked him a question that had baffled me since I met him. "How did you know I was English?"

"In Moscow there are eight million people, and you are the only person wearing shoes like that," he replied, pointing to my feet.

I glanced at my thongs — standard Aussie summer footwear — and laughed out loud. It'd never occurred to me that I could be identified this way. I'd been careful not to wear jeans or other clothing that could mark me as a Westerner, but thongs were a natural extension of my anatomy.

After more laughter and stories, we escaped from the claustrophobia of the rowdy bar and joined the millions on the street. Victor, unknown to me, repeated the cautious behaviour of my guide the previous day by continually checking behind us, but he was so skilled, it didn't register. As we neared my hotel, he said quietly, "We're being followed."

I squashed the desire to glance behind me, but scanned a little to the sides. It seemed to me as if every Russian in Moscow walked the streets, the footpaths so packed that many chose to walk along the gutters. Strangely, the roads were almost empty. Ten lanes wide, they supported only the progress of an occasional government car or bus. It would've been smarter to put pedestrians on the road and vehicles on the footpath!

"How do you know that?" I asked Victor, thinking it impossible to know if anyone watched us from among all those people.

"We are being followed," he repeated with concern in his voice. "A man dressed in a suit wearing a hat is on our tail. He has been following us for a couple of kilometres. In Russia, you always need to watch your back."

"Really?" I gasped, my heart jumping.

"I've got to go," he said quickly. "I'll meet you at nine o'clock outside your hotel tomorrow."

Without waiting for a response, he crossed the road and was

gone, disappearing into the mass of human beings. He left me only one block from my hotel, but I was worried. I continued walking with the crowd towards my hotel, not game enough to turn my head and wondering whether I or my friend was the focus of the surveillance. Maybe the man in the suit had left me to follow Victor. The closer I came to my hotel, the more anxious I became. Not knowing was unbearable.

Half way up the twenty or so magnificent steps which led to the impressive front doors guarding the foyer of my grand hotel, I *had* to know what was happening behind me. Was I being followed, or was my friend severely paranoid? I sat down on a step and casually watched people walking past, searching for the man in the hat and suit. A multitude of men wore hats and suits. How would I know who was the stalker?

Then a man wearing a hat and a suit walked past, stopped and turned around and glanced at me. I casually glanced down and slowly turned the other away. Out of the corner of my eye I saw him retracing his steps. He walked past me for about twenty metres, stopped, turned, and his eyes found me again. Again, I avoided looking directly at him. Using my peripheral vision, I watched him repeat this routine five or six times — walking past, stopping, turning, observing me, retracing his steps for another twenty metres, stopping, turning and watching me. Stunned, I recalled the fear of my imaginary arrest by the Soviet military at the airport, but this was real. Here was clear evidence that I was the subject of surveillance, and surveillance meant KGB. The word *terror* describes my state as I sat on that step. I felt powerless, my mind a mess. Had I been watched from the moment I'd set foot in Moscow? Had there been someone on my tail yesterday who my kind friend from Perm had not detected? Or was I under suspicion because I'd befriended a Russian dissident who'd done time in prison, simply on suspicion of talking with a US journalist? So many questions and no answers.

After recovering from the shock, I had a strange urge to test this dangerous reality. The intelligent, sensible thing to do was to walk up the remaining steps into the foyer of my hotel and go to my room. However, I couldn't let this matter rest. I had to know for certain if I was this man's 'person of interest'. He walked past the bottom of the steps again, and I stood and descended to the footpath, joining the ten-deep crowd swirling past. I turned in the opposite direction to my stalker and walked slowly ahead, imagining that by now he would've completed his twenty-metre routine, be turning and would see me walking away from him. Would he follow me?

I walked on through Red Square, not turning or looking back over my shoulder. I must have travelled at least three blocks before I made a U-turn and headed back towards my hotel. About ten steps later, I spotted him, walking towards me. Unbelievable! Tightness gripped my chest as he approached. I couldn't take my eyes off him. As we passed, I stared at his face, but our eyes never met. He avoided my gaze and walked by. I turned and watched him walk on. This time he didn't turn. He walked on and out of sight. The sinister reality hit me with renewed dread. I felt as though an iron fist had slammed into my stomach.

I'm not sure how I got back to my hotel. Shocked and dazed, I staggered into my room overwhelmed by a thousand thoughts. Was it now a matter of time before the KGB would pick me up? What would I say? Should I come clean about my reason for travel through Moscow? Maybe I needed to contact my parents or go to the Australian Embassy. What about tomorrow and meeting my friend as arranged? Nothing was clear. I'd kept a diary of my trip, committed to writing a page a day—not wise under the circumstances because it contained details of my activities and conversations. If the KGB arrested me, I'd have much explaining to do. It would seal my fate.

On that warm summer's night, I gazed from the window

of my hotel overlooking Red Square, beautifully illuminated by hundreds of lights, until, not knowing what else to do, I began my entry for the day. "I know I should not be writing this …" I began. My writing that evening filled twelve pages.

Chapter Eleven - Dangerous Request

"On the hook of truth only small carp will bite; in the net of falsehood the big salmon are caught."
Latvian Proverb

I didn't sleep well that night. Mum and Dad had warned me not to go on this crazy mission, and one of the reasons was the unrest in Europe, with Russia being the main offender. The Soviet Union was preparing for the Moscow Olympics in June, a month away, with the US and other countries threatening a boycott. The Polish labour strikes were gathering momentum under the leadership of Lech Walesa, a dissident trade union activist, and ripples from Poland were irritating the leadership of countries in the Communist Bloc. (I learnt later that many folk in communist controlled countries, including my uncle in Latvia, listened regularly to the BBC, even though it was illegal and they would have been severely punished if caught.) Latvia, Lithuania, and Estonia were furious with the Soviet decision to send their boys to fight in Afghanistan, to be used as cannon fodder in place of Russian soldiers. When *Operation Eagle Claw* failed — Jimmy Carter's attempt to rescue fifty-two US citizens held as hostages in the US Embassy in Tehran — shock waves rocked the globe, and Russia was the epicentre.

When I woke in the morning, feeling groggy, I decided that now the dust had settled overnight I wouldn't try to contact my parents. It would only confirm their fears if I spoke to them about my predicament. After all, I was still alive. The secret police had not knocked on my door during the night, and the travel tour people had not sought me out. So I decided to keep my appointment with Victor, my Muscovite friend.

I slipped out of my hotel and found Victor waiting a careful distance away. He seemed in good spirits but a little nervous. But everyone in Moscow appeared anxious. An invisible cloud of heaviness hung over the walkers on the streets. Smiles were almost non-existent as the serious masses progressed along the pavement. Victor wanted to expose me to some of the sights, and we headed for the Olympic ski jump course on the top of a hill near the university. The winter snow had melted. The sunny slopes covered with grass had become a playground for summer. I stood beside Victor at the top of the ramp, looking down the dizzy descent over bare boards to the grass below. Young men on grass skis, who had little respect for life, rocketed down the timber ramp at breakneck speed and gracefully sailed around seventy or eighty metres before landing on the grass.

Next, we visited the Moscow metro, which was one of the USSR's most extravagant architectural projects. Stalin ordered the metro's artists and architects to design a structure that embodied 'radiance and brilliance' and a radiant future. With reflective marble walls, high ceilings and grandiose chandeliers, many of Moscow's metro stations have been likened to an artificial underground sun. This underground communist paradise reminded its users that Stalin and his party had delivered something substantial to the people in return for their sacrifices. Proletariat labour had produced this 'svetloe budushchee'.

The escalators disappeared into a bottomless pit. The deepest station lay buried seventy-two metres below ground level. Even though the speed of the escalators was fifty percent faster than most others I'd used, it took some time to travel the distance.

Many commuters comfortably read a book or a newspaper on what could be the fastest moving footways in the world. I negotiated entry and exit from these mechanical death-traps with great concentration and respect. Stations layered one on top of each other under Red Square, crisscrossing to all points of the city. The main line transported around 2,000,000 passengers a day. The platforms were one hundred metres long, and the trains wider than other trains I'd travelled on. Around every forty-five seconds a train stopped, and hundreds fought their way on and off the carriages. The architectural extravagance and the well-maintained cleanliness of each station blew me away. Ornate tiles covered stations not constructed from marble, and some had marble statues for decoration.

Victor was keen for me to visit a Beryozka store, run by the State, which sold goods for hard currency. Goods sold there were unavailable for Soviet citizens, so access was restricted to high-ranking Russian officials, foreign travellers and diplomats. Some Muscovites who used the black market and had accumulated hard currency could not use it in the restricted stores. But stores accessible to Soviets contained few items, often just a few basic vegetables for which desperate folk queued for hours. Beryozka shops stocked a vast array of goods and were usually free of human congestion. I offered to buy Victor something from one of these privileged places, and he asked for mohair wool. The store contained everything imaginable. The Soviet system prized 'one of every kind', but the Beryozka store had a choice of colour and variety that would overwhelm the average Westerner. The Soviets managed with four-foot black umbrellas, yet in front of me sat umbrellas of all colours, sizes, retractable and foldable. I returned to Victor with six balls of his prized wool, which would give much joy to his wife.

"Let's eat," I said to my gracious and grateful guide. "It's my shout."

We made our way across Moscow to a restaurant of Victor's choice. I accepted that I'd already paid for my meals in the cost of the tour, but the extra expense was worth it, and the cost of food was cheap compared with Western prices.

Towards the end of our meal, Victor said, "I've got something to tell you." His manner suddenly changed. He became visibly nervous and unsettled. "I have something on me that no one else can see," he whispered. "If it gets into anyone else's hands, I'm dead."

I stared at him in stunned silence for a moment. "What is it? Tell me."

He glanced around and took a deep breath before continuing. "I know a lot about the Soviet system and have written a book about it. I want to get out of the country, and you're my only chance. I have two chapters on me that I want to get to the Americans. I know that once they read these chapters they'll want to get me out of the country. That's my plan. Also, I have a photograph of myself, my personal details, including address and telephone number. However, if this gets into the wrong hands, I'm dead." His hands shook with nerves. "What I would like you to do is take these two chapters to the US Embassy for me."

Maybe I was a sucker for the underdog. I'd witnessed the discrimination and hardship suffered by Dad in establishing himself in his early years in Australia. I'd been labelled a wog and excluded from games by kids at school. I'd seen what it was like to be on the bottom rung, to be downtrodden and treated like shit. Dad's ill treatment in Nowra had left an indelible mark in me. I hate the abuse of power and will fight for justice. I examined Victor's face, noting the pain in his eyes, the tense jaw. I sat stunned and silent for a minute, my mind racing. Strangely, I didn't think about my mission, my grandmother, or finding my family. Here was a man in need, a victim of an oppressive system causing misery for millions, including my family in Riga.

"Yes, I'll do it," I responded before I had considered the consequences. "How do I get there? Will you come with me?"

He explained that the Soviets banned Russians from going within a kilometre of the American Embassy. He would take me as close as he could to the building, but the rest was up to me. Soviet security was tight around the building.

I nodded. "Let's do it."

He glanced around, checking that no one watched us, then passed the two chapters under the table. I glanced down and noticed it was handwritten. One page contained his contact details and a photograph. I stuffed it down my undies, paid the bill and walked out of the restaurant. Victor gave me clear directions and said he would wait for me at the restaurant. I headed off and instantly became aware of a knot in my stomach. The mercury on the anxiety barometer had risen significantly. I took some comfort from hearing Victor say that he wasn't aware of anyone tailing us. However, the thought of the man with the hat and umbrella sat uncomfortably in my mind. This devious activity could land me in prison and Victor in Siberia, or possibly worse. I couldn't get his words out of my mind, "If anyone finds out, I'm dead." This mission required great caution.

I decided to hide my money belt on the outside of my underwear and place my passport in my pocket, in case I was searched. I walked over to the side of the footpath and stopped momentarily, trying to make the discreet adjustment before continuing my covert operation. The embassy was near Red Square, some distance away, and it took forever, made longer, I suspect, because of my contraband. I wanted this risky business over as quickly as possible. I must have covered two kilometres through the crowded streets before the imposing structure of the US Embassy appeared. As I approached, the crowd thinned significantly, and I became more exposed; no longer could I hide in the masses.

The enormous, white-stone embassy covered a whole block.

Dozens of American flags waved proudly in the breeze. The building was set back a hundred metres from the road in open grounds covered with lawn and trees. Soviet security, there in force, was not difficult to spot. I searched for the main entrance, but many entrances confronted me — too many and with no clear signage. My stomach tightened while I anxiously searched for the right doors. I had to go through the correct entrance. If someone asked me what I was looking for, how would I respond?

I took a deep breath and confidently walked past the first entrance, then the second and the third. The next entrance was larger, so I headed for the open doors. I wasn't aware of any surveillance, but that changed fifty metres from the doors. Without warning, I found myself lifted off the ground for a split-second and dumped back on the pavement. Two burly Soviet guards had grabbed me from behind. They held me firmly on either side.

"What business do you have here?" one guard asked in a heavy Russian accent.

I indicated that I wanted to show my passport, and they released their grip. It gave me a moment to think, and I said the first thought that came into my mind. "I'm an Australian, and I want to emigrate to America."

The knot in my stomach felt like a rock the size of a football. Were they going to search me? If they did, I was gone, and Victor was dead.

The Russian pointed to the entrance ahead. "In there."

I thanked him and walked on, not daring to look over my shoulder. *What a stupid thing to say. I'm a tourist on holiday and wanting to emigrate to the us. What was I thinking?*

As I walked through the doors, the rock in my stomach dissolved. It was a relief to be safe inside the building. In front of me, a young female receptionist sat behind a long, polished wooden counter. A staircase climbed to the first floor on my left, and photos of American presidents lined the walls. I stood behind a guy talking to the receptionist and waited nervously. Two minutes later, he completed his business and moved to one side to organise his documents. The receptionist was busy typing, and I expected any moment for her to finish and ask me how she could help. I glanced down at the papers of the guy standing beside me and noticed CCCP on his passport. He was a Soviet citizen. The sight of his papers shocked me and I began to panic. For a moment, I wondered whether I was in the US Embassy. What was a Russian doing in here? The Soviet authorities prohibited Russians from entering. *If this guy is a Soviet, I can't produce Victor's book in front of him.*

The receptionist fortunately still had her head down absorbed in her typing, so I quietly stole away from the counter and climbed the stairs on my left. They led to a large room on the first floor where photos of Jimmy Carter and other presidents hung on the walls. I walked past the first door and noticed a smartly dressed woman in her early thirties seated behind a large desk between two American flags. She glanced up and said, "Can I help you?"

I walked into her office, and with great relief immediately understood that she was the Consular General. I recounted the details of visiting Moscow, meeting Victor and his plea for help. I told her I had two chapters of his book. She said she'd like to see them. A moment of embarrassment followed. I had the chapters stuffed down the front of my underpants, with my trouser belt strapped tightly around my waist holding it in place. First, I had to undo my belt. I assured her everything was all right — I wasn't up to any funny business — then reached deep into my crotch for the pages. She remained professional throughout my contortions. I handed them over, and she quickly examined the pages, then put them to one side. I asked her where her home was in the US. Coincidentally, on my travel across Canada and the US, I'd stopped in her town in Maine and bought a pie from a shop close to her home. I'm not sure if it was that connection, or she needed a break, but a few minutes later, she asked, "Would you like something to eat or drink?"

Even though I had just finished a three-course meal, I was not going to pass up an opportunity to have a drink with the US Consular General. We walked up the stairs to the cafeteria and sat outside on the deck. I ordered a cup of tea and a small cake, and only then noticed how attractive she was, tall, blonde, intelligent and good-looking. I relaxed and sat with her, enjoying American hospitality overlooking Moscow. This was my reward for undertaking a risky mission.

I spotted the two guards out the front of the embassy and said, "They are Russians?"

"Yes, Russian police."

I frowned, puzzled. "I thought you would have your own police. I didn't think you'd have Russians guarding your embassy."

"It's normal, but if you look across the other side of the street, you'll notice a car with two men in it. They're our security watching the two Russian police. And see that man on the rooftop over there, he belongs to Soviet security, and he's watching our guys watch the Russian police."

She continued to talk about the cat and mouse games played out between the US and the Soviets. The Soviets watched her flat and her, every moment of the day and night. Every afternoon she saw the KGB follow her home and US security men watching them. She said I'd taken an enormous risk bringing the material into the embassy, and I think she considered me a little crazy.

I asked her what the chances were of getting Victor out.

"Russians are given the opportunity to defect, but they have to have good reasons,' she replied. "We have these requests all the time. I'll send this information off to my superiors, and if his information is valuable, we'll get him out, but it needs to be very good."

That day registered high on my anxiety scale. As I look back,

I realise more fully the risk I'd taken. I have no doubt that my impulsive decision to help Victor, and face an even greater threat later, had its roots in the way my father lived his life and my early experiences in work and play. I came away from that day with Victor wondering what made me do it. It was almost a reflex action—a spontaneous act that defied logic when placed alongside my central purpose for the trip. While I'm usually aware of my anxiety, it seldom shuts me down. I have a certain 'comfortability' with danger—something developed when I faced the onslaught of bruising bodies on the football field and when I attempted new challenging skills. Intuitively, I had a good sense of what was required, and from my experiences I gained two valuable assets: my thirst for adventure and being a risk taker.

To this day, I don't know if Victor got out of Russia. I hope he did. He was a good bloke and deserved a break. I gave him my address in case he did make it to Australia, but I didn't take his details. I thanked the American Consular for her generosity and reluctantly walked down the stairs into the embassy grounds. I passed the two Russian guards and found my way back to the restaurant where Victor waited patiently. I felt as if I were walking on air. The KGB had not arrested me. Neither had I been searched. I'd successfully fulfilled my mission and had socialised with the top brass at the embassy.

It had been two hours since I'd left Victor, and his eyes lit up as soon as he saw me. He didn't smile often, but he smiled then. I gave him the feedback from the American Consular, and he seemed encouraged. He thanked me profusely, and I bid farewell. We'd developed quite a bond, and I was sad to leave him, but dusk drew near, and I had to be ready to leave my hotel at seven p.m. to catch an overnight train to Riga.

Chapter Twelve - A Serious Miscalculation

"The mass of men lead lives of quiet desperation."
Henry David Thoreau, Walden

I felt great walking back to my hotel after the exhilarating, satisfying and exhausting day of drama with Victor and the US Embassy. I had two and a half hours before my train left from Moscow Central Railway Station, and I wanted to be sure I arrived in plenty of time to avoid any problems at this most critical part of my trip. Proud of my attention to detail, I walked at a relaxed pace, knowing I'd booked my taxi and paid for it four months previously in Australia. All was going well, until I approached the desk to collect my key.

The receptionist looked up. Her face instantly set and her eyes blazed. "Where have you been?" She fired off those menacing words with the same force and anger I'd experienced previously.

I stared at her and didn't say a word. What could I say? What could be wrong now?

"Where have you been?" she repeated even louder. "You've missed your train. You should have been here an hour ago."

She was angry with me? Why? It took me a minute to work out the problem. My watch told me it was 4.30 p.m., so what was the issue? Then the penny dropped. Unused to thinking in twenty-four hour time, I had seven o'clock fixed in my mind, but the scheduled departure time of my train was 1700 hours — five o'clock. The blood rushed to my head and my heart exploded into a gallop. *I've blown it*, I thought in sheer panic. *After all my careful preparation, I've stuffed up.* I had to pack and then travel to the other side of the city in thirty minutes! After a couple of deep breaths, which provided partial composure, I decided to give it a go. *I'm not going to give up without a fight.*

The taxi driver was standing in the foyer, waiting patiently, a silent spectator of the noisy drama. The receptionist's voice returned to moderate volume but still with an accusatory tone, "You have missed your train; there's nothing you can do."

I picked the key up from the counter and said, "I'm going to pack and will be back in a minute." I raced to my room and stuffed clothes, sleeping bag and tent into my large red backpack and dashed back to the foyer. The patient taxi driver had not moved from the place he'd witnessed the unfolding drama minutes before. He understood English and needed no further explanation.

"It's no use, you'll never make the train in time," the receptionist called after us as the taxi driver took my backpack and ran down the steps to his taxi with me hard on his heels. I ignored her, but her words rang behind me. "Silly man, silly man."

The driver threw my backpack into the boot, and I jumped into the front passenger's seat. It only took the first fifty metres of my journey to understand that the young driver had taken my predicament as his great challenge for the honour and glory of the Communist State. He was going to deliver me to the station even if it killed him, and as it happened, it came close. He accelerated to ninety kilometres an hour.

The streets of Moscow had relatively few cars compared to other major cities, but pedestrian traffic was overwhelming. Traffic lights were few, but countless pedestrian crossings without lights cut across the streets, and every crossing contained an unbroken wall of people. One hundred metres from crossings, my driver leaned on the horn until he'd passed through the pedestrian zone. Some people froze in their tracks, some retreated towards the footpath and others fled to the safety of the opposite pavement. Many times I thought we would kill or maim those poor people. Terrified, I gripped my seat. This young Muscovite was doing his best for me, but while he was a good driver, he was driving well beyond his ability. It was a miracle we finally arrived at the station without death or injury.

The distance from my hotel to the station was much further than I'd imagined, but eventually I saw that one final sharp turn would put us into the railway car park. The speedo showed eighty kilometres per hour as we entered the turn, and the car listed dangerously, tyres screaming. I believed we weren't going to make it, that the car would flip. My aching hands remained firmly riveted to the door and dashboard. The tilting of the taxi, as it strained to perform the impossible, threw me against the door, and it seemed an eternity before the car righted itself. It did so with a force that flung me against the driver. I glanced at him and noticed him breathing heavily. So was I. We found a parking spot and opened the taxi doors to the pungent smell of burning rubber.

"Where's your ticket?" he asked urgently.

I drew it from my pocket; he took a quick look and we ran to the platform. The train was about to leave.

A miracle had been performed! What a relief.

But a new drama was about to unfold. The driver found a conductor who pointed out that my carriage was at the other end of the train. *No problem*, I thought as we walked quickly along the platform. The station was on a slight curve, and I could only see three carriages. We hastened on, and I saw three more carriages, and then another three carriages. The crowded platform became the next threat. Hundreds of passengers with their family and friends barred our progress. I began to jog, ducking and weaving between bodies. The carriages still appeared with no sign of the end. It felt like a nightmare.

We'd travelled an exhausting kilometre when my legs began to tire. I'd not taken the usual care to pack my backpack, so it was uncomfortable and unbalanced. In my haste, I'd stuffed everything in as best I could, thinking I would repack it on the train. Usually, I packed so the weight rested on my hips, but now my shoulders were taking most of the load, and sharp edges dug into my back. I couldn't run because of the weight and the solid frame of the pack, which extended below my backside.

My taxi driver ran ahead, shouting, "Come on, come on."

I wanted to give up. My body ached. I could barely catch a breath, and perspiration dripped off my face. My loyal driver noticed I was flagging, came behind and lifted my backpack, taking the weight off my shoulders. It provided some relief, and we both continued, a comic duo at a fast trot, ducking and dodging between bodies. I sided-stepped to miss a group of people and my poor driver blindly crashed into them, sending them flying. One desperate collision knocked an old woman and a middle-aged man to the ground. We stopped and quickly helped them to their feet, apologising profusely before continuing our awkward choreography along the never-ending platform. I thought, *Russia not only has the longest escalators in the world, they also have the longest trains in the world.* The train was two kilometres long. Later in my travels in the Soviet Bloc, I faced other long-distance trains of a similar size.

We jogged on and on, until it appeared that all passengers had boarded and the train was about to depart. My legs were screaming and ready to give out at any moment.

My long-suffering chauffeur stopped two carriages from the end—unbelievable! "This is it," he gasped.

The celebrations were brief. We stopped and hugged. He was proud *we* had made it. I gave him a generous tip and boarded.

When I glanced back out the window, he was still standing there, smiling and breathing heavily as the train moved forward. I waved and walked down the passageway to find my compartment. I opened the door, noted the two bench seats facing each other and the small cupboard in the corner, then collapsed on one of the seats, exhausted, breathless and lamenting my confusion with timekeeping.

And so I headed northwest to Riga and sacred ground—Latvian soil. This tiny jewel of a country, situated in north-western Europe on the eastern shores of the Baltic Sea, lies opposite Sweden, south of Finland and Estonia, and north of Poland and Lithuania. It covers 65,000 square kilometres and is roughly the same size as the Republic of Ireland, West Virginia in America and Tasmania in Australia. Its capital city is Riga, which straddles the river Daugava, not far from its mouth where it empties into the Gulf of Riga. The population has never numbered more than 2,000,000 and has survived over 700 hundred years of foreign oppression and serfdom. It has emerged from the ashes of two world wars and the disintegration of the Tsarist Empire with its spirit unbroken and with an astounding degree of viability. Today, it's a modern and prosperous nation—a member of NATO and the European Union.

The train stopped, and a middle-aged man in a suit entered my compartment. He was rather plump and bald with greying tufts of hair above his ears. "Do you mind if I sit here?" he asked, looking over his gold-rimmed glasses.

"Not at all," I replied.

He sat opposite with a leather briefcase resting on the seat beside him. After a few minutes he asked, "Where are you from?"

"I'm doing some travelling, and my next stop is Riga." I hoped he wouldn't ask where the rest of my group were and was cautious about developing conversation with him, so I unzipped my backpack and took out a magazine.

115

"I own a bookshop in Riga. Just visited family and on my way to Rezekne," he said, before I had time to open it.

I'd heard of Rezekne in the heart of Lalgalia in Eastern Latvia. Its Blue Lake, ancient buildings and green fields attract many tourists. I assumed this fellow was Latvian, but if so, how was he able to move around the country so freely? "I'm Australian and have just been to Moscow. I think I'll enjoy Riga more, though. Moscow was very crowded," I offered cautiously.

"Ah, you're Australian. Do you know about Latvia?"

"Only what I've read in travel magazines," I lied, knowing he was keen to talk. That was all he needed to launch into a history lesson on Latvia.

"Latvians or Letts belong to ethnic group of Balts, who settled on the south-eastern shores of the Baltic Sea about 4,000 years ago. Balts split into tribes. Eventually, only two tribes surviving — the modern Latvians and Lithuanians. Latvian and Lithuanian are among the most ancient living Indo-European languages — they came from ancient Sanskrit."

"I had no idea," I interjected.

Without missing a beat, he continued. "Archaeology shows at beginning of the twelfth century they had a high level of civilisation and extensive trade with foreign merchants, including Greeks, Scandinavians, Romans, Russians, Arabs and even Phoenicians. In the thirteenth century, German Crusaders brought destruction and oppression. Though they said they bring Christianity to pagan people, their real objective was to conquer Latvia. Despite fierce defence of their land, the Latvian kingdom was overwhelmed in 1290, partly due to the skill of the invading Germans and partly due to conflict among the tribes."

I was most impressed by his knowledge. "You certainly know your history."

"I should. I was a history teacher in my earlier days."

"Your English is also very good," I commented.

He laughed. "Thank you. I also taught a little English too

and I can tell you it's the most difficult language I have ever tried to learn."

"What made you change to bookselling?" I asked.

"I love reading. I could read books every day and then sell them. I save lots of money doing it this way." He laughed, and his whole body shook. "I have a good life, and the authorities give me freedom to move around because of my business. But let me tell you a little more of my history."

I was happy to listen. While in schoolteacher mode, he wasn't asking me questions about my visit, and I found him interesting and his delivery eloquent. Obviously, he'd done it many times before. I wondered if he'd spent time in England.

"Do you know that Latvians had to wait for over 600 years for restoration of independence? They had to endure oppression, serfdom, and hard times from many wars and plagues before a sovereign Latvian State could be established. The territory of Latvia with its plains, gentle rolling hills, forests, beautiful lakes and the ice-free Baltic ports of Kurzeme became a hunting ground. Many foreign peoples wanted Latvia — Germans, Danes, Swedes, Poles and Russians. Parts of Latvia came under the rule of the Polish and Lithuanian kings. Kurzeme became autonomous Dutchy of Courland under Poland. It was the last of the areas of Latvia to be taken over by Russia at the end of the eighteenth century. The opening of the nineteenth century found the entire territory of Latvia under Russian rule."

This character was like a talking encyclopedia, so concise, so eloquent. As he spoke, my eyes revisited his clothing — a well-cut suit of good material. It fitted his bulging body awkwardly. The brown leather briefcase, I guessed, was not a cheap item; neither were his highly-polished leather shoes. This man was certainly not living on the poverty line. The more I tried to make sense of this character, the more the uneasiness intensified. He continued with my history lesson:

"Despite centuries of oppression and conflict, Latvians

managed to survive as hardworking peasants. They clung … ah, very strongly to their traditions and culture and always tried to improve their education. Some Russian aristocracy and especially clergy had a more … what's the word … enlightened view and helped the indigenous population. This helped a dramatic awakening of my people in the nineteenth century. By the beginning of the twentieth century, Latvia and Estonia were educationally the most advanced areas of Russia and had the lowest rate of illiteracy."

"That's amazing. I never realised that. They obviously were very strong-minded."

"They certainly are very determined. Latvians survived all attempts to make them Russian, even though before the First World War their secondary and higher education had to be done … acquired, I should say, in Russian or German. Latvians managed to ensure Latvian finally came into its own language of literature and instruction."

I nodded. "You must be very proud of your people who have survived so well."

"Oh, yes," he smiled. "And the struggle continued. On 11th August, 1920, the Peace Treaty was signed between Russia and Latvia. The Latvian Provisional Government then worked hard in establishing relationships with foreign countries and making laws over every area of national life. Russia and Germany still oppressed, but nationals from these countries, including Poles and Jews and other minority groups, were given the right to all democratic privileges. It included education for their children in their own minority languages. This legislation was unique in European history."

"That was very generous of Latvia, very generous," I offered.

"Yes, most certainly. The Latvian political leadership brought financial stability and prosperity to Latvia, which had been invaded from either side of its borders by Russia and Germany. The Constitution, which provided for significant social reforms, including voting with equal rights for men and women, was passed on 15th February, 1922. Also, any group of five or more Latvian citizens aged over twenty-one had the right to form a political party."

"That's amazing. A very generous recognition of the different interest groups and ethnic minorities in Latvia," I interjected. It was difficult to get a word in.

"Yes, exactly, but it contributed to frequent changes of government. That was the downside. Despite these political difficulties, Latvia continued to make headway — economically, socially and culturally." He paused to take a swig from a hipflask produced from his coat pocket. "Like some?"

"No, thanks."

"This next period of my people's history is distressing for me." He looked down at the floor and lowered his voice. "The world economic crisis in the early thirties had a devastating impact on most European economies, including Germany. The impact flowed on to Latvia. Russian and German military attitudes excited their nationals living in Latvia, and Nazi youth organisations emerged, including a right-wing Latvian group called Thundercross who were intolerant of other nationalities, including Germans and Jews. The communist underground in Latvia received a flood of instructions from Russia, preparing for Soviet takeover. A state of emergency was declared in Latvia on 15th May, 1934, and Latvian authorities introduced proposals to stabilise the political system by reducing the number of parties. The Prime Minister, Karlis Ulmanis, was very respected. His strong leadership proved a real effort to restore stability. A modified form of representative government was re-introduced, including some nationalisation of property."

"That must have been a scary time," I reflected. Then I remembered Dad's lifestyle before war broke out in 1939 and I wanted to show some intelligence, so I asked, "Did that give Latvia an economic boost?"

"It most certainly did," he replied, as he looked at his watch. "Agriculture was made more modern. The electrical industry flourished. Did you know the world's first Minox camera, the smallest camera in the world, was developed in Latvia?" Before I had time to answer, he continued. "Latvia produced locomotives, railway rolling stock and light aircraft. The textile industry and other industries began to produce export goods on a large scale. This era saw national health schemes developed and good pensions for workers and employees. Cultural life flourished — music, the arts, literature, theatre, ballet and the opera. Education reached high standards. Even under the authoritarian government, all national minorities continued to enjoy freedom in education, religious practices and all basic and civic rights. Latvia was enjoying a time of prosperity when Soviet forces invaded on 17th June, 1940. Ulmanis courageously didn't desert his post. He was arrested and deported to Russia, where he later died."

He raised his chin as if in defiance, obviously filled with pride of his country's history. "I'm proud I'm Latvian. It's not easy living under the Soviets, but I make the best of it." The train at that moment began to slow. "Ah, this will be Rezekne. You will be in Riga. You are very welcome to visit my shop." He handed me his card.

"Thank you. I've enjoyed hearing about Latvia."

He smiled and picked up his briefcase. "Now don't forget to look me up in Riga later in the week."

"Thank you for the invitation."

He nodded and staggered a little as the train eased to a stop. I made a decision then not to renew contact in Riga.

I sat for a few minutes, reflecting on our meeting. What did he mean by 'It's not easy living under the Soviets, but I make the best of it?' The unease vanished from my stomach, but energy fired my brain. Could this friendly, likeable, well-educated bookseller be a member of the Communist Party? He obviously had a permit to travel, was not short of a rouble, and gave ample evidence he didn't suffer from lack of food. Uncle John was offered membership of the Communist Party because of his business success, refused and was sent to Siberia. It left me wondering, but I never knew for certain if this friendly bookseller had crossed the political line.

The conversation with the bookshop owner confirmed everything my father had told me. I was proud to be Latvian. In some strange way, I was glad I could experience sitting under the Soviet shadow that covered Latvia. I could share a little of what my family and fellow countrymen suffered. That shadow tried to destroy the colour and vibrancy of the people, but never succeeded. Hidden under the heavy grey blanket of communism, the richness and vitality of my people was preserved. Like amber hidden in the soil, only to re-emerge refined and enriched by the brutal forces that threatened to extinguish it.

Chapter Thirteen - Who is That Man?

"No matter how much you eat, save some seeds for sowing."
Latvian Proverb

A great sense of pride filled me as I watched the countryside roll past. This was the land of my forefathers, whose stories resonated within me—stories of suffering and bravery, of hardship and daring. I had not slept well, yet woke excited and alert for whatever the day might bring. Today, I would meet my grandmother and family. That was my hope. The countryside flowed past—open fields covered with crops, newly harvested, wheat stacked in rows, not a machine or mechanical device in sight. All crops were cut by scythe and sickle and stacked by hand. I remember a photo on the front page of the *Moscow Times* of a farmer who'd won a medal for breaking the record for the most wheat cut in a day. The communist hierarchy regularly used these efforts as a means of propaganda, urging everyone to aspire to the selected worker's high achievements.

I was keen to capture these rural scenes on film, but there was one small problem. A sign in the compartment warned 'no photos'. Every half-hour or so, a conductor opened the compartment door and checked to see if everything was in order. I couldn't risk taking a photo with him looking in at the critical moment. However, I wasn't going to allow this once-in-a-lifetime opportunity to pass, so I searched around and found a wire coat-hanger in the cupboard. The next time after the conductor opened and closed the door, I wired the door shut and took photos of the countryside through the window. I unwired it just before he returned for his regular surveillance. The train was due to arrive in Riga at ten a.m., three hours away, and I became aware of a growing anxiety about what might be ahead.

I walked down the corridor to stretch my legs and breathed more easily when I found that my tour companions from Moscow were nowhere in sight. It seemed rather strange. Surely we would be grouped together on the train? Maybe they had paid more for their tickets and were in a classier carriage? I had no idea. I tried to make sense of how I'd successfully managed to remain independent from the group. I'd continually expected a knock on the door of my Moscow hotel asking where I'd been, but nobody had checked on my absence from the group. It was all rather strange. For a moment, I lamented the effort of waking at four a.m. to clean the Woolworth's store between five and eight in the morning. That six-month effort was a waste of time and money! Then I reminded myself that a registered tour group was the only way I, or any other foreigner, could get access to travel inside the Soviet Union. The only way to Riga for me was through Moscow. That was the price I had to pay.

An uneasy thought did go through my mind: Was I under surveillance and not aware of it? Was it part of the KGB's plan to watch where I went and who I met? Another, more immediate concern, grew in my mind. Would I be able to find my grand-mother, uncle and family? I had the directions from Dad's cousin in Canada. My diary held the location in code. If I did find them, would it create problems if I visited? Some neighbours were on the lookout for opportunities to score points with the KGB by reporting anything suspicious. The sudden appearance of a Westerner in a Latvian home was newsworthy, the return of a young Latvian male to his family, more so. I counted myself fortunate to have flown under the radar so successfully. However, there was still the potential for danger in the next three days in Riga.

Victor had reinforced everything I understood about Soviet policy. The Soviets treat Latvian tourists visiting their own country with suspicion. They are potential troublemakers. Their movement in Latvia is greatly restricted. Apart from Riga, they're allowed to visit a limited number of resorts outside the city, and they cannot travel throughout Latvia as foreign tourists can in the United States, Canada or Britain. Latvian tourists from the West are not allowed to come in their own cars and cannot enter Latvia from Poland or Lithuania. They usually travel through Moscow or Leningrad. They are prohibited to bring in books or other kinds of literature published abroad—Western publications are regarded as anti-Soviet propaganda. They are free to take pictures only of 'nice places' and 'nice people' as selected by Intourist, the State-controlled agency.

The KGB can arrest a tourist of Latvian origin for any reason or no reason at all and hold them in police custody for a period without official charge. They are usually held in complete isolation. Communication with the outside world is not allowed. Two years before my visit, Laimonis Niedre, a Latvian of Swedish nationality, was locked up while in Tallinn, the Estonian capital, and kept without trial until the autumn, then he was charged with spying. The Soviets sentenced him to ten years' hard labour. His crime had been taking photographs of Latvia's scenery, ruined churches and farmsteads. In April 1979, only five months after the sentence was passed, Soviet authorities released Niedre on humanitarian grounds and allowed him to return to Sweden. I assume that Niedre's release was because of the wide publicity given to his case in the West and his worsening health, which might have led to his death in a Soviet prison.

My stomach tightened as the train eased its way into the long platform in Riga. Would security challenge me? I touched my money belt, hidden under my shirt, which held my passport, collected my backpack and stepped off the train onto the platform. Friends and relatives greeted the travellers as they poured out of the huge carriages.

"Peter." Startled, I spun my head to search for the man who had spoken my name. How would anyone know me here? Nobody would be aware of my arrival. I stood bewildered, speechless.

"Peter, Peter Jirgens?" he repeated.

A man stepped out of the crowd and smiled at me. Who was this guy?

"I, Uncle John," he said, extending his hand with a smile.

I shook his hand, studying his face carefully, and recognised him from a photo sent to Dad from his cousin in Canada. I learned later that Dad's cousin had mailed a letter to my uncle John in code, telling him of my arrival date and time. This was a special moment; I was finally making contact with my family. Instant relief soothed my body. We hugged briefly and walked towards the exit.

He spoke little English, but enough for me to understand. He and my grandmother were overjoyed with my visit. He said little and suggested we part company. I wasn't sure why but presumed he was being careful. Eyes could be watching. I'd already pre-booked and paid for a taxi, so I bid him farewell and took the taxi to my hotel and checked in. I didn't see the tour group anywhere and, naturally, didn't make any enquiries. I never saw them again.

I pulled out the map Dad's cousin in Sudbury had drawn for me and refreshed my mind with the directions in my diary, then I headed out of the hotel. I saw the markets and the bridge over the river and walked a couple of blocks until I stood outside the family home. The timber house, like many in the street, was in desperate need of repair. The front door sat right on the edge of the footpath, and the house shared common walls with the houses either side. I knocked on the door, and it opened almost instantly. It seemed that everyone was expectantly waiting for my arrival.

My uncle stood there with a great smile, and we hugged again. My round-faced grandmother sat smiling on a bed, her big eyes glistening with joy. I recognised her from a photograph my parents had at home, and knew that she'd retired from work the previous year at eighty-one. She hugged me for ages with tears streaming down her face. My aunt Inara and cousin Peter arrived and welcomed me warmly. They had little English, but we managed to make ourselves understood.

I asked Uncle John how he knew it was me at the station, but he couldn't understand what I said. At this point, Zoja, a neighbour and friend of the family, entered. She spoke very good English and interpreted for most of the time I was there.

Zoja said, "Your uncle John received a photograph from your mother some time ago, and when he shook your hand, he said he knew instantly, because all Jirgens have big hands."

My grandmother cried the duration of my stay. I asked Zoja on the second day why my grandmother was still crying, and she said it was because, "I had arrived." On the third and final day in Riga, I asked Zoja again why my grandmother was crying and she said, "Because you are leaving."

Over those three days I collected, first-hand, many stories related by my Dad during my youth. They included the account of when my grandmother and uncle protested against the Russian invasion after the war. They were forcibly removed from their home in the early hours of the morning and transported in cattle trucks to Siberia. Currently, my uncle was the manager of the largest department store in Riga, but he was still poor. There was no running water in the house. They used buckets to collect drinking water from a nearby facility. Grey paint covered the interior of the house and added to the dreary surroundings. A small fuel stove stood in one corner and a porcelain sink with a single tap in the other. Around the dingy walls, shelves displayed Australian artefacts sent by my parents. My reaction was sadness, and I made a promise to myself, I would give everything I had to them before I left. My uncle wouldn't accept any money, so I secretly left it with my cousin, who gave it to my uncle after I left. During my stay, I asked whether he had received the shoes Dad had sent from Australia. He had not received any shoes.

The days are long in the Latvian summer; the sun sets around 12.30 a.m. and rises at 5.30 a.m. With this amount of sunlight and good rain, crops were plentiful and contributed to a prosperous economy. After the war, the authorities allowed my uncle to have a small plot of ground the size of twenty square metres outside Riga. He travelled by train each weekend and tended strawberries, which he sold to help supplement his income. Included in his entrepreneurial efforts were strawberry jam and strawberry wine made in a room in his home. Hundreds of Latvians were given this concession. His neighbour raised chickens on his allotted plot, and so bartering allowed for the exchange of strawberries for smoked chicken. During my visits, I tasted the best smoked chicken that ever crossed my lips. Sensational!

Everyone worked together cooperatively to survive. Because of the harsh winters when nothing grew—except the depth of snow on the ground—people put great effort and time into preserving their summer produce. During the Soviet-controlled years, Latvians ate a little better than most Russians.

My uncle John, cousin Peter and I walked the streets of Riga. We visited the large port and the busy transport hub. Thousands of Soviet and foreign ships call into Riga every year. The central railway station, airport and sea terminal are pathways into the city. Uncle John produced a magazine that gave me an idea of what the city produced: diesel engines, radios, telephone exchanges, scooters, washing machines, furniture, magnificent knitwear and coffee sets. The aromas from Dzintar's perfumery factory were too overpowering for me. However, the confectionery from Laima and the famous Black Balsam of Riga scored high on my approval list. The instruments made at the Avtoelectropribor plant were exported to all corners of the globe.

I read a publication that described Riga as a city of advanced science, culture and art. The research institutes of The Latvian Academy of Sciences situated here deal with fundamental problems of energetics, organic synthesis, the biology and the chemistry of timber and computing technology and electronics. A good deal of attention is given to the problems of marine geology, textiles, plant protection and the rational use of fish resources in the Baltic basin. Latvia was on the cutting edge of technology.

Chapter Fourteen - Riga

"In history, a great volume is unrolled for our instruction,
drawing the materials of future wisdom from the past errors
and infirmities of mankind."
Edmund Burke

The following day, Uncle John took me to see more sights of the city. We walked everywhere — the beach at Riga, the markets, St Peter's Cathedral, parks and museums. Later in the morning, we headed down towards the river, passing Kirova Park and the Grand Hall of the Latvian State University. We crossed the Pilsetas Canal that winds its way through the ancient buildings and walked past the huge Central Bookstore where small groups of young people congregated outside. I'd discarded the piece of paper containing the address of the bookshop owner I'd met on the train, but wondered if it was his place. Latvians love to read, and there was no shortage of bookstores and libraries in the city.

The road narrowed as we passed the Central Department Store, and soon we stood on the steps of St Peter's Cathedral. This stunning building has a unique 120 metre tower. At nine a.m. and noon, and then every three hours, the tower clock chimes the rousing melody of Riga Dimd, a Latvian folk song. The tower held the record for the tallest timber structure in Europe. The Germans bombed it during the war, fearing Latvians might use it as an observation post, but it was rebuilt after the war. Uncle and I took the lift to the observation landing, which provides an excellent panoramic view of the city. My uncle beckoned me to climb it, and though he saved his energy for the rest of the day, I climbed to the top of the tower and gazed out the small window.

Below, the large shingled dome reflected the afternoon sun, and people on the pavement were tiny specks in the distance. I marvelled at the original structure. The timber scaffolding it would have needed during construction was an engineering feat in itself. A huge rooster perched on the top of a ten-metre pole keeps watch over Riga.

After I descended, we wandered along the old cobblestones to Dom Cathedral, described in the Soviet tour guide as a museum. Its construction began in 1211 and was completed after many changes in the middle of the eighteenth century. It features different styles: Romanesque, Gothic, Renaissance, Baroque and Classicism. The monastery, with vaulted cloister and relics of its ancient past, adjoins the cathedral, adding an aura of romance and uniqueness. Unfortunately, we didn't have the opportunity to enjoy a performance by the magnificent pipe organ in the cathedral. The music of Bach, Handel, Mozart and Beethoven, as well as present-day Latvian and Russian composers, entertain visitors.

Nearby is the Jura church built in 1202 and later turned into a storehouse. This structure connected with my engineering brain. Boulders, bricks and limestone form the walls, and five to seven tiers divide the inner structure. A steep tiled roof completes this ancient masterpiece. A couple of dozen buildings similar to The Storehouse stand in the same street. In earlier times, it was usual to hang the figure of an outlandish bird or beast over the main entrance to a storehouse. Since medieval buildings were not numbered, it functioned as an emblem and an address at the same time. Storehouses were referred to as 'the Elephant Storehouse' or 'the Blue Pigeon Storehouse' and so on. After lunch, we walked past the Gunpowder or Sand Tower, one of the twenty-eight towers of the Riga fortifications. We also visited the Swedish Gates, the only surviving gates of the old city.

One of my favourite buildings was Riga Castle, built in the fourteenth century. I loved it, and so did my uncle. He smiled and gave me the thumbs up sign as we approached. It was once a formidable fortress of the Livonian Order, and as I wandered the passageways, I fantasised about the days of old, swords, suits of armour, bows and arrows. It now holds the Young Pioneer Club. After school, young people come to the old castle to engage in all kinds of cultural activities, including singing and dancing.

It was late in the afternoon when I said goodbye to uncle and walked back to my accommodation. I would have preferred to stay with my family, but that was out of the question. Even though it was more relaxed in Riga, I never lost the feeling of being followed. Throughout the day, I found myself casually checking to see who was behind me. The dread of the man with the hat and the umbrella was emotionally imprinted within. My hotel in Old Riga was clean but drab. It was only for tourists, to preserve the 'purity' of communist ideology and avoid the stain of Western contamination in the city and throughout the country. Everything in Riga was grey.

* * *

The next morning, within minutes of my arrival at my grandmother's home, Zoja was sitting on a kitchen chair while I sipped tea. I guessed she noticed my arrival. Zoja was a wonderful neighbour, friendly and well-educated. Not only did she translate for my grandmother and uncle, but she also related some of the culture and traditions of Latvia.

"I'm sure your father has told you about our rich folklore," she began, patting the chair beside her in invitation.

"He did," I said, as I sat, ready to listen.

"Good, but did you know that even though Latvia is mainly Christian, we keep many of the old pagan traditions alive today?"

I shook my head, and she proceeded to fill the gap in my education.

"The summer solstice is on the 23rd and 24th June, that's Līgo and Jāņi. I think this holiday is celebrated in Latvia as widely as New Year's Eve is in Australia and other countries. We celebrate by dragging the Yuletide log around Old Riga, followed by dancing and singing, and then we burn the log on a bonfire. It's called the night of the Yuletide log."

I smiled. "I haven't heard that one before."

"Yes, it sounds rather strange, doesn't it, but it symbolises getting rid of all things negative. In February, we celebrate *Meteņi*, and in spring, of course, there's Easter, where we have egg-cracking wars and swinging on the Easter swing. People also share in *ķekatas* like mumming."

"Mumming?"

"It's a rhythmic wailing sound made from the throat. You hear it in the northern Scandinavian countries and in Latvia on summer solstice during Jāņi. People light bonfires on almost every hilltop and sing Līgo songs. It's quite wonderful; the sound resonates across the landscape." She paused a moment to accept a cup of tea from grandmother.

I said nothing, just waited for her to continue this enjoyable cultural education.

"Then there's Masļeņica, an Orthodox holiday at the end of winter, seven days before the big fast. It's when the market and kiosk counters buckle under the weight of all kinds of sweets. The most important part, though, is pancakes and dressing-up in costumes. My husband and I love this part of the celebrations. Many folk wrap themselves up in large furs from head to toe."

I wanted to return someday and experience these festivals and to bring Dad with me. How he would love it.

"I understand your father is a great musician and songwriter," she went on. "Do you know that hundreds of Latvian *dainas* or folk songs are still sung today? I don't think there's anything like them in the world. *Dainas* have four-line verses, which are impossible to translate precisely into other languages. They're lyrical, witty and philosophical, containing thousand-year-old wisdoms. The Cabinet of Folk Songs contains over two million *dainas* and is Latvia's national treasure."

I was suitably impressed, and research I did later revealed that UNESCO had included it in its list of Man's Spoken and Nonmaterial Culture.

"One of the highlights for me," she continued, "is the Song and Dance Festivals. They've been going on every four years since 1873. Latvian amateur dance and choir groups from all over the world come here to join a giant mixed choir or perform folk dances. Visitors say they haven't seen anything like it in the world."

I was glad to tell her that Dad continued to play the piano accordion and other instruments and longed for the great Song and Dance Festivals. "He's upset that Australia doesn't have anything similar. We don't have national celebrations of cultural music," I lamented.

Chapter Fifteen - Leningrad

"The duality of St Petersburg and Leningrad remains. They are not even on speaking terms."
Joseph Wechberg

Emotion filled my three days in Riga. The time raced by faster than the three days I spent in Moscow. Not a minute was wasted. If I was not walking the streets with my uncle, I sat chatting with my cousin, family and Zoja, or consoling poor grandmother. It was not easy saying goodbye. Before I left, I offered my uncle money, but he refused it. I placed the remaining American dollars and some roubles in an envelope as a gift for my uncle. I also provided him with my denim jacket, which totalled seven months wages. He was the manager of the largest department store in Riga but still poor. I slipped the envelope to my cousin and told him to give it to his father after I left. My grandmother could not go with us to the station because of her medical condition. It was an emotional departure for us both. She had not stopped crying the three days I spent in Riga, but now the tears were fuller and ran even more freely. I felt so sorry for her. She had suffered so much over the years, and I understood how much family meant to her. Uncle John and Peter farewelled me from Riga station with hugs and more than a few tears. I made a commitment to myself that one day I would return with my Dad. Of that, I was certain.

The train trip to the third city in 'occupied territory' was uneventful. I loved Leningrad, finding the lakes and waterways—canals lined with trees, reminiscent of Venice—impressive. Opposite my hotel room, the ship where Lenin fired the first shots to commemorate the beginning of the revolution in 1918 lay anchored. Banners such as 'glory to the communist party central committee' lined the streets, and the empty roads, crowded trams and overflowing footpaths reminded me of Moscow. People disappeared from the streets after ten p.m. Hundreds of drama theatres and a prolific number of museums and concert halls catered for the cultural needs of the locals.

The Great Palace was striking. I walked along the grey cobblestones and admired the richly decorated facades and the iconic columns. In a moment of excitement, I stopped a young German tourist and asked him to photograph me in front of the massive iron gates that guarded the entrance. The park, once a formal garden built for Peter the Great, still has more than eighty of the original marble statues, sculptures and houses. I could not resist touching these beautifully crafted figures. Peter's Summer Palace is a simply designed two-storey building that displays many of the ruler's own artefacts. I wandered for over an hour overwhelmed by the detail and the extravagance. Spectacular fountains showcase the gardens and, inside, the mosaics rival the Palace of Versailles. The Hermitage Museum is one of the most famous art museums in the world and found in the Winter Palace. Two hours passed in a flash as I marvelled at the works of Leonardo da Vinci, Michelangelo and countless other great artists. I had not seen anything of this kind before. It was a feast for the eyes.

One place high on my agenda was The Church of Our Saviour of Spilled Blood, a beautiful gold-draped, onion-domed church on Griboedova Canal, one of the many waterways in the old Russian capital. I had read about this place in my travel notes. The Russian emperor Alexander II—called the Liberator because he abolished serfdom—was assassinated on the site on 1ˢᵗ March 1881. After the revolution in 1917, the new government closed the church and wanted to demolish it, and it was used as a morgue, then as a warehouse during World War II. What caught my attention was that in 1961 they found a high-explosive bomb in the central cupola of the church—an unexploded Nazi bomb that had been sitting inside the church for eighteen years. It was carefully removed and destroyed. I asked the attendant to point me to the place where it was located. He smiled at my macabre fascination.

One afternoon, I stood in a street lined with modern buildings when an old-timer sitting on a seat beside a dirty fountain asked, "You visiting?" He had a strong accent but I could understand him.

I turned to face him. "Yes, I'm from Australia."

He nodded and smiled. "You not realise it but Leningrad still bears the scars of the terrible Blockade."

"What do you mean?" I asked.

"You wouldn't recognise this place if you'd lived here before war. There were wooden houses here but destroyed in the siege, used for firewood to keep families alive." He looked down at his scruffy shoes and said nothing more.

"It must have been a terrible time," I said.

After a long silence, he looked up and responded. "My sister is a ballet teacher, and she said she has to teach her young students how to smile. The Blockade has taken away happiness from many of our people. It's like a sickness that goes on and on. We have long way to go to get better."

He remained silent and didn't look up again, no doubt buried in the past. I became painfully aware that I could only touch history from the distance of time, whereas he'd lived through it and survived. I felt as if I were walking on holy ground[3]. I thanked him and moved quietly away.

On my last day in Soviet territory, I had thirty roubles left in my pocket. While wandering near the port, I found my way to a pub where some English-speaking Soviet university students were conversing noisily. I set up camp with them and shouted drinks for the rest of the afternoon. For a couple of hours, I was the most popular patron in the pub.

One of the students had problems reading, so I took him down the road to a shop that had tables full of second-hand reading glasses. There didn't appear to be any optometrists in Leningrad, and if they existed, I suspect the average citizen wouldn't have been able to afford the cost of a pair of glasses. The procedure was very simple. Customers tried the glasses on until they found an acceptable pair. Gradually, my new friend worked his way through a dozen or so until he found a pair that worked. I could tell they suited him because of the smile on his face. I paid for them and felt humbled by his gratitude. We returned to the pub where the celebrations and conversation continued throughout the afternoon.

"You have dangerous snakes in Australia, don't you?" one of the students asked.

"Yes. Where I live, we have brown snakes that are highly venomous."

"Have you ever been bitten?"

"No, but there's a story about my brother that is worth hearing." At that moment, everyone turned their full attention on me. I took a swig from my beer and launched into one of my favourite stories.

"My close shave came during a two-day surveying job in thick bush, when I almost trod on a six-foot black snake. I hate snakes. Strangely enough, I went home for lunch and Mum told me there was a parcel for me from my brother John who was travelling overseas in South Africa. I opened the parcel and rolled out the contents. It was a python skin, twenty-two foot long, nearly seven metres, and twenty-two inches wide, which made its diameter around seven inches." I showed with my hands the breadth of the snake and received appropriate gasps from the boys. "It was like leather with two eye holes in it. This was a massive snake. Unbelievable! The enclosed letter gave the story.

"Peter, John's mate, and John were walking along a jungle trail towards a village when a boa dropped from a tree. Peter told John that he kept snakes back home and that this one wasn't dangerous. He told John he'd try to catch it and have a closer look, but John had seen enough and sprinted up the track. John could hear Peter scrambling through the bush, and a few minutes later, he heard him scream. John grabbed a thick piece of wood and ran back along the track. Peter was kneeling on the snake's neck while the snake wrapped itself around his body. His hand was caught in the snake's mouth, and the ugly creature began crushing him. Peter told John to strike the snake across its back, a foot from its tail. When he struck the snake a few hard blows, it began to quiver and released its deadly grip. While helping Peter get away, John almost collapsed from shock." Everyone sat motionless, drinks firmly anchored on the table.

"The two of them continued on to the village and came across a native who spoke broken English. They told him of their close call, and the native offered to skin the boa for a packet of cigarettes and three dollars Australian." I paused for a moment.

"That's some story," one of the boys said.

"It's not finished yet. I told a few footy mates, and word got to the local newspaper. The next minute, I had a reporter on my doorstep wanting me to show him the snakeskin and the letter. I draped the skin over the clothesline and across the backyard. A photo of the snakeskin and the story appeared on the front page of the newspaper the following week. It was big news in the town. A year or so later when John returned home, my mother gave him the newspaper clipping about the snakeskin. John read it and laughed.

"What's so funny?" I asked.

"I made it up," he replied.

A roar of laughter rose from the group. Many more beers lubricated my tongue that afternoon, and so more stories followed. At the end of my grand social occasion, I had few roubles left but many new friends.

What a way to finish my three cities tour. I'll never forget that afternoon. Afterward, I returned to my accommodation and prepared for the following day's train trip from Leningrad across the border into Finland. It was to be one of the scariest times of my entire trip — an unforgettable experience. Little did I know that my departure from Russia would be far more traumatic than my entry.

* * *

Early morning arrived, and I found my way to Leningrad station, walked along the never-ending platform and boarded the train for Helsinki. I located my compartment with ease and found myself seated with two middle-aged Finnish women who were returning to Helsinki from Leningrad. The taller woman, who I estimated was in her mid to late forties, had soft eyes, greying hair and a lined face that indicated that life might have been difficult for many years. Her younger and plumper friend had a quick smile and bright eyes.

The train moved slowly from the platform and gradually picked up speed. I pulled out a magazine and read while the women talked incessantly in their own language. After about half an hour, the younger woman asked, "You're not from around here, are you?"

"No, I'm on a trip. I'm Australian. I hitchhiked through Canada and had a few days in Moscow, Riga and Leningrad."

"Oh, that sounds wonderful," the older lady said in a soft voice tinged with sadness. I wondered what her story was.

I glanced out the window and observed a flock of cormorants

flying leisurely towards the sea. "Do you have cormorants in Australia?" she asked.

"Yes, they live on the coast where I live. I love watching them dive for fish," I replied.

"I have a friend who travelled through Australia some years ago," the older woman said, "and she loved your native birds. She said they were so colourful."

The scenery didn't capture my attention, and I enjoyed their company, so was content to continue the conversation. "I used to have a galah for a pet."

"What colour is a galah?"

"Pink and grey. They're very intelligent and live in country areas in Australia. Sometimes, in school holidays, my brother John and I went with Dad to his jobs when he worked out in Western New South Wales. On one occasion we spent a few days helping Dad dig irrigation drains on a property on the Murrumbidgee River, and when we'd done our work, we amused ourselves building traps to catch crayfish. On the day he planned to return home, Dad picked up an injured galah on the side of the road. It'd been hit by a vehicle while it fed on wheat spilt by trucks transporting grain to the silos. Dad placed the galah in a box, and we took it home.

"It survived with plenty of tender loving care. I built a cage, which later expanded in size when John decided to keep pigeons. I let my galah out each morning to fly around in the open before I went to school. Later, I'd call him back and make sure the gate of the cage was closed. I named him 'EE-EE' after the sound he made. He always returned within … maybe thirty seconds when I called his name. He'd sit on my shoulder and eat from my hand. Even when he was hundreds of metres from home—just a grey and pink speck in the distance—I'd call his name and immediately he'd fly back and land on my shoulder."

"That's amazing to have a wild bird do that," said the older woman.

"He loved my finger stroking his comb. Within seconds, he'd fall asleep and then suddenly wake up with a start as much as to say 'What's going on here?' He was a character—we were close buddies."

"So you tamed a wild bird, how amazing!" the younger woman said, her eyes wide.

I nodded. "I had a rather embarrassing incident one day, though. When I was fourteen, I broke my ankle playing football. For weeks, I hobbled on crutches with plaster up to my knee. I couldn't ride my bike to school and had to take the bus. One morning, while walking with a friend to the bus stop, some distance from home, I heard 'ee–ee'. I looked up and there was my galah, cheekily sitting on the power lines. I called him down, but because my friend was beside me, EE-EE wouldn't budge. "Go home," I shouted, but he still sat there, making his distinctive call. I realized that in my haste to catch the bus, I'd forgotten to return him to the cage before I left home. As we walked on to the bus top, EE-EE walked along the power lines above us. I kept pleading, 'EE-EE, go home, go home', but he wouldn't obey."

"It sounds like this was going to be a problem for you," laughed the older lady, obviously enjoying the story.

"Yes, it was. I clambered onto the bus—a new experience for me since I'd previously always ridden my bike—and arranged myself as best I could to ensure kids wouldn't fall over my plastered leg. Eventually, the bus stopped outside the school, and I walked to the top of the stairs to exit the bus and hesitated. I'd never done stairs with crutches before. Gingerly, I leant forward, placed the crutches on the step, slowly transferred my weight and managed the first step. So far, so good. Another step and then again I heard, 'ee-ee'.

"I glanced up and saw my galah sitting on the power lines. I almost fell down the stairs with surprise. He'd followed me all the way to school. Exercising great care and patience, I managed to get down the steps onto the footpath. The next challenge was to catch EE-EE. I called him many times to come and sit on my shoulder, but with other kids around, he wouldn't risk it. He then went berserk, resembling a skilled fighter plane zooming around the playground. He swooped low over the heads of kids, some screaming with delight, others ducking in terror. Under covered ways, under trees, around the playground seats he buzzed to the sounds of squealing and screaming children. Kids yelled, 'Watch out, it's a galah.'"

Both women smiled, clearly enjoying the story. "What happened next?" the younger woman asked.

"EE-EE didn't slow down and continued his screeching and high-speed aerobatics. I'd never seen him behave this way. He became everybody's focus before the bell rang to go in for lessons. And it didn't stop when we were in class. Through the window, I watched EE-EE rocket around the buildings, two metres above the ground screeching, 'ee-ee'. All the kids were going feral, and I was most embarrassed. Two or three periods later, I received a call to go to the principal's office. Mr Sykes was a great principal, but I'd never met him—until now. What a way to meet him! I grabbed my crutches and nervously hobbled to his office.

"He called me in right away, and I lowered myself onto the chair facing his imposing desk. 'Peter, is that your galah flying around the school?' he asked, peering at me from beneath his bushy eyebrows. 'Yes, sir,' I replied. He smiled just a little, as trying to hide his amusement. 'Well, Peter, you'll need to take it home.' I swallowed before replying, 'I can't, sir.' He looked at my crutches and nodded. 'Yes, well, I'll organise a taxi for you.'

"Soon after leaving the principal's office, I was sitting in the taxi with EE-EE safely perched on my shoulder, heading for home. One good outcome of the morning's events—I gained half a day off school."

The younger woman laughed. "That was clever of you!"

I stopped for a moment and became aware of a knot in my stomach. I couldn't make sense of it. Why was I feeling anxious? There was nothing suspicious about these two women. I felt at ease and relaxed with them. I loved telling stories, and they seemed happy to hear them. I dismissed my anxiety and continued the conversation.

"How old were you at this time?" the younger woman asked.

"I would've been fourteen. I remember around this time I overheard that the pet shop in town was selling galahs for twenty dollars a pair, which to me was a small fortune. My brother John and I decided to trap some galahs using EE-EE's presence and persuasive personality and sell them to the pet shop owner. I sectioned off a small part at the front of EE-EE's specially-made cage with a trapdoor connected to a fishing line that ran to the kitchen window. I sprinkled sunflower seeds on the floor of my new trap and waited at the kitchen window, the end of the fishing line in hand, ready for my first customer to arrive. This was the humble beginning of what I believed to be a profitable enterprise."

"You are very creative," the older woman said with a laugh.

"It didn't take too long before a galah appeared and cautiously waddled into the cage to eat the seed. Quickly, I pulled the fishing line, closing the door. I handed the line to Mum to hold, grabbed a pair of plastic gloves and a box and headed for the cage. By this time, the feathered victim was squawking loudly, letting me know he wasn't happy about his confinement. Now, you're not familiar with galahs, but it's important to understand that their beaks are extremely strong. They hang from branches by them and can crunch their way through branches the size of my finger with ease. I should've factored this into my approach as I opened the door of the cage, because when I seized my feathered prisoner, its bolt-cutting beak went CRUNCH. It cut neatly through the glove, straight to the bone. Instant pain, instant blood and instant release of my prospective twenty dollars."

The younger woman laughed, then blushed with embarrassment and covered her mouth. "Oh, I'm sorry I laughed. That must have been very painful?"

"Yes, it was. I was fortunate not to have lost a finger. My new enterprise finished at that exact moment."

"So you never captured any birds and never made any money?"

"That's right. One day, EE-EE went away for twelve months. He was out of the cage for his early morning freedom flight, when he joined a bunch of galahs and disappeared. I was devastated and, for months, whenever I saw a galah I'd call out, 'Ee-ee, ee-ee.'

"About twelve months later, two galahs flew past the back of our place. I called out, 'Ee-ee, ee-ee,' and one galah peeled off, flew down and sat on a branch of a tree. The other circled and landed beside it. "Ee-ee, ee-ee," sounded from the first galah. "Ee-ee, ee-ee," I responded. It was my bird."

"How amazing," the women said in unison.

"I opened the door of the cage, which had been closed for months, and placed seed on the floor. Immediately EE-EE flew down and began eating. He was hungry. It seemed like he'd not eaten for six months, the way he shovelled seed into his belly. I kept the door of the cage open, allowing him to fly off or for the other bird to join him. The other bird sat quietly in the tree for four hours before it finally flew off. EE-EE seemed content to be home and the old rituals continued. He stayed with me for another twelve months before he flew off again. Then, six months later, when I was doing my paper run after school, struggling up the hill on my bike, fully laden with papers, I heard that familiar sound, Ee-ee, ee-ee. I looked up and couldn't believe it. Here was EE-EE. He'd recognised me even when flying thirty metres above. He flew down onto my shoulder, and we completed the paper run together. He accompanied me home and lived in his cage for another two years before he died."

"That's a great story," the lady with the sad eyes said. "Did you ever find any other wounded animals?"

"The only other time I can recall was from that same stretch of road near the Murrumbidgee River, a year later. This time it was a baby kangaroo. A vehicle had hit the mother. Dad took the little joey from its pouch and gave it to me. I sat in the back seat of our car for the return trip home with the joey curled up under my jumper. We fed him for a couple of weeks and then he died."

"That was sad," the younger woman said quietly.

"Well, maybe that was good because he was a Big Red. Goodness knows what dramas may have happened if he'd reached maturity!"

Chapter Sixteen - Unexpected Danger

"There are times when fear is good. It must keep its watchful place at the heart's controls."
Aeschylus

The subject then moved to kangaroos and koalas until the knot tightened again in my stomach. What was going on with me? I sat with the feeling for a few minutes. Inspired by my story-telling, the women asked more questions about Australia. But I needed a break. I excused myself, walked into the passageway and found the toilet. Gradually, the problem dawned on me. I was so caught up with talking about EE that I'd forgotten about the border crossing. I calculated that we weren't far from it. I returned to my compartment and became increasingly anxious—a strange feeling. What could go wrong? I couldn't make sense of it. My papers were in order. My fear on entry into the USSR had been imaginary and proved baseless. Little did I know as we approached the border that my growing fear was well-founded. My instinct was soon to be proved correct.

Lack of sleep, mixed with the pace and excitement of my time in Riga may have contributed to the uneasiness that crept into my body. In the silence of the compartment, interrupted by an occasional comment from the two women, my mind turned again to the threat that hung over me. I'd explored the three cities and completed my mission, and was grateful I'd not suffered detainment by the authorities. It seemed too good to be true that I'd made it safely through the Soviet State. The absence of follow-up by the tour company when I was AWOL still puzzled me. I had no explanation about how I'd so successfully avoided detection.

As the countryside rolled past, my anxiety continued to grow. Mild panic crept into my body and refused to leave. I wanted to be over the border and into the safety of the West, instantly. The checkpoint could not come quickly enough. In a heavily forested area I asked the two women how far it was to the border.

"Thirty kilometres."

Anxiety probably distorted my perception, but the long train seemed to be going even slower. I asked again a little later, "How far now?"

"Three or four kilometres," came the patient reply.

Instant relief. 'I've made it,' I thought. Minutes later, the train slowed until it finally stopped. I jumped up, slid the compartment door open and walked into the passageway, where I could open a window. I poked my head out. Heavily wooded forest enclosed the track on both sides. The only sign of civilisation was a house with smoke rising from its chimney set back about a hundred metres from the railway line. Strange.

On an overhead walking bridge above the train lines, Soviet soldiers stood looking down on the roof of the train — a sight that did not sit well with me. Even stranger, below them in a long concrete trench beneath the rails, a handful of soldiers stood inspecting the undercarriage. The train moved on at a walking pace and the soldiers examined every carriage. Once the last carriage passed over the trench, the train stopped.

My anxiety intensified even further when I observed soldiers entering the train; dozens of them, some with German shepherd dogs. I scrambled back to my compartment, where the women were chatting amiably. I heard the soldiers' heavy footsteps marching up the passageway. The compartment door flew open, and an impressive-looking officer in his forties strode in.

"Passports," he demanded. We handed them over, and he examined the women's documents first, then mine. "You leave," he said, looking at the two women, then he pointed at me. "You stay."

The Finnish women gave me a concerned look, grabbed their bags and left the compartment.

The officer moved on to the next compartment, and I sat alone, aware that fear had again taken hold of me. A minute later, a young soldier in his mid-twenties opened the door, placed his machine gun in the corner and then stepped up onto the seat. He produced a screwdriver and removed six or seven screws from the ceiling panel. The panel dropped down and the soldier rested it against the seat and then began to search the cavity with a torch. I said nothing, just sat nervously anchored to the seat. What was this bloke on about? After replacing the panel, he sat down opposite me, resting his gun against his right knee.

"Your papers." The command came with a heavy accent. I handed over my documents, and he inspected them carefully, examining every page. "Empty backpack."

I emptied the contents onto the seat. Sleeping bag, tent, toiletries, clothes, everything came out. He unrolled and carefully examined the tent and the sleeping bag. Nothing escaped his scrutiny. My uncle had given me a porcelain bottle of Balsam with a wax top, Latvia's national drink, made from nineteen herbs and spices and forty-five per cent proof. For over 200 years it was used as a medicine and is now a highly-prized beverage. My uncle wanted me to hand it to my Dad. "He'll remember this drink," he'd said with a smile. Each day I'd painstakingly wrapped the Balsam in my towel and placed it in the centre of my backpack. The soldier pointed to the bottle.

"Where did you get this from?" Before I could answer, he continued, "Where is your money?"

Then it dawned on me. I had to declare everything when I

entered the USSR. They were all recorded in my papers. How was I going to explain where my 350 US dollars went? What could I say about the expensive bottle of Balsam? I had no supporting documentation for it. He pointed to the two spoons given to me by the generous Russian family on the first night in Moscow. "Where did you get these?"

"The Russians are generous people. They give me presents," I offered quickly.

He returned the money. "Where are your American dollars?"

The only receipt I had was for the twenty roubles I'd received when I first landed in Moscow. It was illegal to use the black market, where, of course, no receipts were issued. The authorities required visitors to use the Russian banks, where the rate was one rouble for one US dollar. I was in trouble.

Careful not to give any indication of the panic in my body, I responded with calculated confidence. "The weather has been good in Riga," I offered with a smile.

He didn't appear to understand any of my responses, probably because of my accent, though I could understand his English, despite his Russian brogue. I continued to rave on about the weather while he stared at me, bewildered. Finally, he stood up, and with my passport in his hand, said, "I not understand what you say. I get my boss. He speaks it well."

Those words hit my stomach like shrapnel. His boss could speak English well! I imagined that the officer he referred to was the one who'd first appeared in the compartment. He'd addressed the women in Finnish, and I'd overheard him speaking various languages to travellers in the adjoining compartments. He was obviously competent in many languages. If he came to interrogate me, I was in trouble, big trouble. I could talk rubbish to this soldier, but I'd be finished if the officer appeared.

My heart raced, but I steadied myself, smiled occasionally and confidently kept good eye contact with my confused interrogator.

He picked up his submachine gun and slung it over his shoulder. I stood up also. As I think back, I can't believe what I did next. He moved to the door and I grabbed his left arm. It was a stupid thing to do, I know. I risked arrest for crossing the boundary, but it seemed the only thing left for me to do. "You have my passport," I pleaded.

"It's okay. I speak to my boss. I cannot understand you."

"You can't take my passport," I pleaded more urgently.

"I need to talk to my boss."

The struggle went on for a couple of minutes while I gripped his arm. If he left the compartment, I was done for. It would've been all over for me. I was beside myself, and my panic had become obvious. "It's my passport. It's my passport."

I don't know what made him sit down again, but he did. He laid his gun across his knees and searched my paperwork again. I relaxed a little and resumed my ranting about the weather and anything that came to mind. He sat bewildered among my belongings strewn over the seat, shuffling my papers, while I confidently prattled on, orchestrating an occasional smile at the right moment. Finally, he shrugged his shoulders, handed my passport back, slung the gun over his shoulder and walked out of the compartment.

Drained by the experience, I didn't move, just sat and stared at my belongings and listened to his footsteps moving down the passageway. Would he return? Eventually, the train slowly moved forward. Relief washed over me. Whenever I retell this incident, I still feel fear. I was so fortunate not to have been hauled before the authorities where, with further investigation, the status of my nationality would've been discovered. Not until the train had moved many kilometres from the border did I find the strength to repack my belongings.

Chapter Seventeen - Mysterious Detour

"A single gentle rain makes the grass many shades greener. So our prospects brighten on the influx of better thoughts. We should be blessed if we lived in the present always, and took advantage of every accident that befell us."
Henry David Thoreau, Walden.

The rest of my journey was uneventful, thank goodness. I arrived at Helsinki and booked into a youth hostel located inside a sports stadium. Only then did I realise how tired I was.

Every day I went to the markets and bought bread to have with the huge block of cheese I'd mistakenly purchased in Moscow. I'd lined up outside the shop with everyone else, and when I finally reached the counter, I'd ordered bread and cheese—or so I thought. The staff member gave me a ticket showing the cost of the item, and I queued again to pay for the goods. Eventually, I walked out of the shop with a massive block of cheese, the size of a loaf of bread, but no bread. Weird. And confusing. And I had to cart this huge hunk of cheese around with me. I made it my mission in Helsinki to reduce its size before I left the city. Every day I bought bread and a little salami and walked down to a park beside a lake to enjoy my cheap meal. Then I lay down on the grass and slept solidly throughout the day. Late in the afternoon, I would wake, realising I'd been asleep for five or six hours.

I repeated this same pattern for three days in Helsinki — the same grass under the same tree, yet I slept uninterrupted every night in the youth hostel. Exhaustion gripped me. The excitement, drama and lack of sleep of the previous weeks had physically and emotionally drained me. In Helsinki I felt safe and relieved, and I just wanted to lie down. Every bone in my body ached. I had achieved my mission, well beyond my wildest expectations. My fears of arrest by Soviet authorities, the anxiety of possibly not finding my grandmother and family or not being able to communicate with them, managing transport and a dozen other concerns had gone. I could relax, and relax I did, sleeping sixteen hours every day for four days.

Only one day had a change of pace. I sat on the seats and watched contestants in the World Frisbee Championships perform fabulous feats with their plastic saucers.

I spent time reflecting on my Latvian experience and writing in my journal. My visit to Dad's past brought life to the stories he told around the dinner table and when we drove together to his work sites. It gave meaning to who he was and why he did what he did. My forefathers were like most Latvians: survivors, determined and driven to succeed. They were creative, honest, fair-minded, hardworking people who loved the land. Experimenters who lived on their wits and took risks, often walking close to the edge to survive. My visit allowed me to see and touch the rock from which my father was formed. John, Julie and I are chiselled from the same stone. I spent time plotting how I might be able to get Dad to return to Latvia. If I could do it without any major strife, maybe he could also. That became my next challenge.

* * *

After resting in Helsinki, I grew thirsty for more adventure, and the next stage of my journey took me north into the Scandinavian regions, then through Germany and other parts of Europe. Little did I know that I would face unexpected danger and narrowly escape death.

I began by hitchhiking north into Finland. One memorable day in the north of Finland, close to the Arctic Circle, a Finnish fellow gave me a lift. He couldn't speak any English, and I couldn't understand him. After months of hitchhiking, I'd developed a good sense of people and an accurate early warning radar about them. I couldn't put my finger on the cause of my unease with this man, but the longer he drove, the more it grew.

When he turned off the highway onto a bush track, my radar went into full alert. He motioned that he wanted me to go with him. I shook my head, said, "No," and pointed back to the main road, but he ignored me and drove on. Where was he going, and more importantly, what was he going to do with me? I wondered if he was a serial killer like Ivan Milat, who'd preyed on backpackers in New South Wales. We drove through the middle of nowhere. Though a big smile creased his face, and he appeared to be friendly, I became increasingly concerned. I searched the landscape, trying to take in any significant landmarks, and became hyperaware of my surroundings and his body language.

He drove further down the bush track until we reached an old homestead. The white-painted farmhouse had successfully survived the elements over many years but had been deserted for some time. He opened the car door and motioned for me to follow. By this time, I was on red alert and prepared for anything. I could survive the worst anyone dished out on the footy field, and I believed I could handle this character if he was up to no good. He walked towards the house through the long grass, and I followed a few measured paces behind him. What was he up to? He turned to check I was following and signalled me on. We turned the corner of the house and the reason for his diversion became apparent. I almost laughed with relief. Dozens of cages were stacked beside the house, filled with minks. We walked between the cages, and I gasped at the enormity of the sight. Hundreds and hundreds of these beautiful little creatures stared at me from their cages. He produced meat and invited me to help him feed the animals. We spent over an hour with the minks and then returned to the car and found our way back to the main road along the bush track.

A short distance further along the main road, still in the middle of nowhere with not a sign of civilisation about, he stopped the car and signalled for me to get out. By this time I was more comfortable with him, and the stoppage aroused more curiosity than fear. Smiling broadly, he tried to tell me something. He pointed to a pile of rocks by the side of the road and conveyed that I should be happy, that I had accomplished something, but the rocks didn't mean anything to me. In response to my confusion, he pointed to a spot on the map I held in my hand. Then the penny dropped. This was the Arctic Circle. I nodded and smiled, and he laughed. I had made it. To celebrate, I spent a few minutes creating my own pile of rocks and he took a photo as evidence of this grand achievement.

A day later, another Finnish guy picked me up on the road. He also didn't speak a word of English. I don't think any of my drivers in Finland did. He seemed a little unsettled and cautious, but of course, he had no idea who I was, where I had come from or where I was going, so I opened my backpack and pulled out an Australian flag. He smiled then and relaxed.

We drove through a region covered with beautiful lakes. He pointed out a side road, and we left the highway, heading for the top of a spectacular mountain. A short time later, we stood together at a popular visitor's attraction, a lookout on the top of the peak, overlooking the magnificent waters. A sizeable car park provided parking for the lookout and a small café nearby. My driver disappeared into the café, returned with a pie and gave it to me. I accepted it gratefully. He then walked over to a group of people

Item(s) checked out to p11077578.

TITLE: Flight of the Conchords.
BARCODE: 30568000831883
DUE DATE: 02-13-19

TITLE: Double negative
BARCODE: 30532004750333
DUE DATE: 02-13-19

TITLE: This one's for him : a tribute to
BARCODE: 30684001188536
DUE DATE: 02-13-19

TITLE: The dreamers : a novel
BARCODE: 30386002596960
DUE DATE: 02-13-19

Call the Hudson Library 715-386-3101
    or visit hudsonpubliclibrary.org

in the car park and returned with a woman, who said, "This man wants me to tell you this is the Finnish national dish — fish pie."

Kalakukko is made from whitebait mixed with bacon and other ingredients, and it's delicious. I smiled at my generous host and thanked him. He seemed pleased that I liked it.

These kinds of experiences added spice to my day. I could never predict from one day to the next what was going to happen, and no matter what happened, it usually turned out well for me. I revelled in the glorious unexpected and became intoxicated with the thrill of spontaneity.

I'd always wanted to go to Hammerfest, the world's northernmost town at seventy degrees north. It's the oldest town in northern Norway and historically a strategic port. I stood looking out over the harbour while one of the locals provided me with a historical commentary. During the Napoleonic Wars, Great Britain attacked Denmark, and Norway was forced into the conflict on the side of Napoleon and France. As one of the main centres of commerce and transport in Western Finnmark, Hammerfest became a natural target of the Royal Navy's blockading warships. In 1809, the expected British attack came when the *Snake and Fancy* approached the town. Before reaching Hammerfest, the British vessels had looted the village of Hasvik, laying waste to the small fishing community. The following battle between Hammerfest's two two-cannon batteries and the British warships with thirty-two cannons was surprisingly intense. It didn't end before the Norwegian cannons had run out of gunpowder after about ninety minutes of combat. Both attacking warships suffered many cannonball hits. Each had at least one fatal casualty. During the battle, the local populace had been able to escape with most of the town's goods, but the raiding warships remained in the port of Hammerfest for eight days. During their stay, the Royal Navy sailors looted all they could get their hands on, including the church donation box and some of the church's silver. The local who related the story was a volunteer in the visitor's centre. Her fair skin was wrinkled, probably from too many cigarettes, but the sparkle in her eye intrigued me.

She told me that in 1891 Hammerfest was the first town in Norway and northern Europe to introduce electric streetlights. The polar bear is on the town's coat of arms and is a symbol of the town's roots, connected to Arctic hunting. She said Hammerfest is a great jumping-off point to explore the mountains, the sea and the mountain plains, no matter what the season. It's the land of the midnight sun, where the sun never sets during the summer months. I embraced the northern part of Norway, filling my lungs with clean, crisp air. I felt enlivened and formed the belief that I could overcome any problem in life.

Hammerfest gives a spectacular view of the Northern Lights from autumn to spring when the Aurora lights are at their most frequent. To see the Lights, it needs to be dark and cold with as little cloud as possible. They say Mother Nature's Light Show involves 400km/sec solar winds. Between ninety to 500 kilometres above the earth's surface, ribbons of green, red, blue and purple can be seen rippling across the sky. They gather momentum until the Northern Lights shimmer and loop over the entire horizon in surreal swathes of colour.

I regretted missing the Night Lights and promised myself I would return one day and see them. Even without them, though, Norway was spectacular—crisp, green forests mixed with aqua blue ocean and pristine white icecaps. I witnessed an abundance of wildlife and tasted the red king crab from Barents Sea off the coast of Finnmark—delicious.

I met some of the Sami, Norway's indigenous inhabitants, also known as the Reindeer People. Their language, traditional clothing, handicraft and music are distinctively different from any other ethnic groups in Scandinavia. In Norway, over forty native communities draw most of the family's income from reindeer herding in a habitat constantly shrinking due to mining, clear-felling the forest and construction of hydroelectric power plants. Samis usually have at least one family member or relative who is in some way involved with reindeers. The reindeers are still fundamental to their culture and society.

Being the most northern town in Norway, 1500 kilometres north of the Arctic Circle, Hammerfest was cold. The temperature fell to minus seventeen degrees. I didn't want to get caught out hitchhiking in the middle of nowhere and be forced to camp out — my sleeping bag was only rated to minus one. So I decided to hitchhike south, down through the Norwegian Fjords to Berlin and then later to Munich. I gazed in awe at the spectacular fjords that cut through tall mountains, had waterfalls cascading down their sides, glaciers that never melt at their head and clear blue skies above.

Not far from Valldal, a friendly group of Telecom workers chatted with me and soon discovered I was an Australian. One technician asked, "What's your home number?" A few minutes later, he returned and said, "Your mother is on the phone."

"Really?" I took the phone. "Hello, Mum."

"Is that really you, Peter?" The line was crystal clear.

"Yes, Mum, it's me."

"It can't be. The line is so good, it sounds like you're just next door."

"Mum, I'm up in the north of Norway, and some Telecom workers have allowed me to talk with you for free."

Silence for a moment, then, "John, will you stop playing around and wasting my time."

"Mum, it's not John, it's Peter. Fair dinkum!"

The line went dead. She'd hung up on me. I'd been the victim of brother John's reputation as a great practical joker.

MAR 1962

1929: Arnold's parents Emma & Janis Jirgens (back, left to right), with Arnold & Janis Jirgens in front.

WWII: Arnold Jirgens playing piano accordion while in the
American army.

Germany after WWII: Arnold Jirgens standing on the kegs with
the piano accordion.

A drawing from Arnold Jirgens' Journal

A page from Arnold's Journal

Pages from Arnold Jirgens' Journal

Hand drawn map from Arnold Jirgens' Journal of his journey
to Australia.

Chapter Eighteen - A Brush with Fame

"All men want, not something to do with, but something to do, or rather something to be."
Henry David Thoreau, Walden

The existence of the Berlin wall meant that to get to Berlin, I had to go through East Germany. Locals advised it was not wise to hitchhike into Berlin because of the heavy police presence on the roads. Bus or trains were the recommended form of transport. Berlin is right in the middle of West Germany, and police were always searching cars for East Germans trying to escape to the West. Police cars guarded every exit into Berlin from the major roads through East Germany.

A German bloke on his way to Berlin picked me up. It was fortunate for me but, as it turned out, not so fortunate for him. At the border of East Germany, a black comedy unfolded. I could not speak German. My kind driver could not speak any English. The guards didn't speak English. I understood enough from the guard's gestures to realise that my German friend could not explain who I was and what I was doing in his car. The frustrated guards ordered him out of his vehicle and told him to stand to one side. I watched in horror as the two suspicious border guards stripped the car of everything; even the seats and the lining in the roof. They jacked the car up, crawled underneath and painstakingly examined every part. I was so embarrassed and sorry for this poor bloke who stood there stunned by the arrogance and belligerence of the guards. Cars rolled past, but we still stood silent, humiliated. It took over an hour for the guards to be satisfied that no contraband items were on us or in the car. To add insult to the terrible ordeal, my long-suffering driver and I had to restore the seats, panels and parts of the interior, stripped by the guards in their aggressive but fruitless search. I felt so guilty. The driver would've had an uneventful crossing if I'd not been in the car.

I loved Berlin and stayed for a week, during which I made some calls to book accommodation for my next stopover — Munich and the October beer festival. I rang youth hostels, caravan parks and a range of low-cost accommodation in Munich with no success. Only the expensive hotels still had vacancies, but at 100 dollars a night, I decided I'd chance finding somewhere once I got there. I found my way to the autobahn on the outskirts of West Berlin and waited for a lift to Munich. A film producer picked me up. Thus began an incredible experience, a dream and a nightmare rolled into one.

My generous German driver, Gerd Jaubowski, lived with his wife in Munich. A well-known film producer, he was currently working on a Rainer Fassbinder film called *Lilli Marlene*. I'd seen his previous film, *Midnight Express* — a brilliant, scary movie — in Australia. He'd just spent three months in Poland shooting *Lilli Marlene* and had booked the Deustches Studios in Munich for a month to complete the filming. Lilli Marlene, a famous singer during World War II, had captivated the hearts of soldiers from every nation on every battleground, including the USA, Germany, France, Britain and Australia.

Gerd fascinated me, and I think he found me interesting. He invited me to stay at his house in Munich, and, of course, I accepted. As soon as we landed at his home, his wife asked if I had any washing, and I gladly emptied my bag. She immediately set to work on my grubby clothes, impregnated with dirt from Soviet streets. We enjoyed a meal, and then came the question which changed the course of my journey, "Would you like to come down to the studio tomorrow?"

What an opportunity! I couldn't refuse. I explained I had some banking to do first and agreed to meet him at lunchtime. When I arrived at the studios at midday, security ushered me through to a large pool, complete with ships and a submarine. Workers were energetically painting scenes — little houses, a sunset and other figures — on large sheets to be used for filming that night. Finally, I found my friend in his office, and he told me what was happening on the set. Someone came into the office and said they were short of an extra. My friend turned to me and said, "Would you like a job?"

I didn't hesitate to accept the offer, and I soon found myself standing in the wardrobe department wearing a Scottish uniform, backpack and shouldering a rifle. Next stop, makeup. I emerged with a blackened face and was sent to the trenches. A backhoe had been digging a trench during the day, and I climbed in along with six others. We sat listening to Lilli Marlene while a camera mounted on a narrow-gauge railway line panned our faces. The camera focused on me as I sat pensively soaking up Lillis' voice, then it moved on to capture an Englishman sitting in his trench, also soothed by the same voice — all of us, captivated, tuned-in, seduced by Lilli Marlene. That was how it happened in the trenches. That was the first day on the set.

On the way home, Gerd said he was moving on to a fight scene the following day, where Lilli Marlene sings in a Cabaret to a large audience. The scene was set before the outbreak of World War II and involved two British soldiers listening to Lilli Marlene. Twenty German SS troops sat in the crowd and would end up in a brawl with the two British soldiers, who eventually would triumph over the Germans. The key figure in the scene was Bob, one of the best stuntmen in Europe and organiser of the fight. The Germans were making the film for the English market, so the English had to win. When he told me that, I laughed, wondering how the German actors would feel.

He offered me a job as an extra, which I willingly accepted. I was to work as a German soldier with twenty experienced part-time actors—unbelievable! During the following days, I had moments when I questioned the sanity of my impulsive decision.

I presented myself at the appointed hour along with eighteen burly Germans who'd gathered on the set, ready to be selected, hoping to make their mark and get even greater roles in the future. They talked and joked among themselves, but with no idea of the language, I had no sense of what they were saying. They could have being paying me out for all I knew. A fit-looking character walked in and nobody took any notice of him. The chatter among the mob continued as he walked over to a table, but his next move took my breath away. In a flash, he leapt onto the table, then somersaulted off, landed with a loud thud on the concrete floor and then jumped to his feet. This was Bob's way of introducing himself. The talking stopped immediately. He had everyone's attention. This guy had presence. He also had black belts in multiple codes and commanded big money as the best stuntman in Europe. Now he was going to select a partner to work with from the assembled brawn of twenty part-time hopefuls.

He walked up to me and said something in German.

I shook my head and indicated that I didn't understand.

He repeated the same words again.

"I don't speak the Deutsch," I said.

"Ah," he replied, "an Englishman. Hit me."

I frowned, puzzled. "You want me to hit you?"

"Yes, hit me," he replied, pointing to his chin.

I stood motionless as I tried to make sense of his directive. *He's only a little bloke. Why would he want me to hit him?*

"Hit me, hit me," he repeated, frustration creeping into his voice.

I asked him at least four times whether he really wanted me to hit him.

"Yah, yah, hit me, hit me," he shouted impatiently.

Still anxious and not understanding why, I shaped up and threw my best left-hand punch. He knocked my hand to one side, grabbed my arm and sent me crashing onto the table, then off onto the floor on the other side. It happened so quickly that I hardly knew what'd struck me. I struggled to my feet, hearing the Germans jabbering among themselves. Next, he called up a German and tried something different with him. For the next three hours, he continued to engage every individual in the group with various bruising moves. He left the room for a minute and returned with a German man. They walked over to me, and the stuntman's companion said, "He wants you to be his partner. This will mean you'll receive an actor's pay rather than an extra." I could hardly believe my ears. Without hesitation, I said, "I'll do it."

That's when the real fun started.

We rehearsed the scene for three days. My task was to take out eight Germans, and he would take out the remaining twelve in a fight scene among 150 screaming people. The scene opened with Lilli Marlene singing on stage. One of the soldiers began heckling her, and a soldier beside him said, "Give the lady a chance." The heckler then kicked this soldier off his chair and laid into him as he struggled to his feet. My part was to pick up a wine bottle and smash it over this bloke's head, but I was concerned about breaking his head open. It seemed like a normal wine bottle—I had no idea it was made from sugar—so I was a little unsure of undertaking such a vicious assault. In broken English, Bob insisted that I do it, so I prepared myself. In my nervousness, I squeezed the bottle too tightly, and it exploded into a thousand pieces.

The director came over, frustrated that I'd blown the scene

and necessitated a clean-up before trying again. "Don't do that," he repeated several times.

I felt somewhat shattered too.

After sweeping up the scattered sugar, we shaped up for a second take. This time I held the bottle loosely, brought it down on the skull of the belligerent soldier and it successfully shattered into a cloud of fake glass. The victim of the impressive blow staggered convincingly around while two SS guards rushed towards me. They seized me from either side, and complete with top hat, bow tie, tuxedo, pocket-handkerchief and pointy shoes, I fought back with suitable force. The scene continued with the groggy soldier, covered in sugar glass, pounding my stomach with his fists, while the two SS guards held my arms. On the fourth blow, I lifted my legs and pushed my attacker through a glass window. Then I called up my strength and catapulted the SS guard on my right through an open door. That's two gone. The SS guard on my left was my next victim. Being a strong man from the West, I picked him up and hit him. He cooperated with a backward roll across the stage and out of sight ... three down and five to go.

It took three days of bumps and bruises to get the action to a level which satisfied the director. It was full on, but I loved it, and best of all, I was being paid good money. One by one, I continued to deal with the determined brawny soldiers as they charged, intent on wiping me out. Finally, only one soldier remained, the one who'd continually caused me grief. I was kneeling, having successfully disposed of my seventh victim, when my final assailant, a little guy, rushed in with a baton, intent on breaking it over my head. In rehearsal, we practised my right hand shooting up under his arm and my left hand grabbing his hip. He helped my impressive lift with a small jump, and I hoisted him above my head and then bought him down with significant force, breaking his back over my right knee. Then I'd throw him to the floor and finish him off with a few forceful punches for good measure.

This precarious manoeuvre came at a critical part of the scene as the intensity builds to the finale. The first time he ran in during rehearsal, I didn't have the correct hold and he fell to the floor and rolled around in agony. He couldn't speak English, and I couldn't speak German, but I hoped he might at least understand my pleading, "I'm sorry, I'm sorry."

Another occasion when I was learning how to control his fall as I brought his back down over my knee, my knee ended up in the small of his back with great force. Again he writhed around on the floor in agony. I responded with greater concern, "I'm sorry, I'm sorry."

I was nervous about the last part of the scene. For three days, we practised every move at least ten times. This was a significant production involving big money and over 150 actors, dozens of crew, make-up artists and others. I felt inadequate, especially partnering the top stuntman in Europe. I thought, *I shouldn't be here. I'm the new boy on the block.* Stuffing this up was not an option, but to get the fight with the last character right was a real challenge for me. Fortunately, he was small, which helped.

In the final moments of the scene, my last long-suffering victim came to the door and stopped. What was he doing? He was supposed to keep running and try to hit me over the head with his baton. I decided to get to my feet, and I stood for a moment thinking they may want to get some footage from the six cameras carefully hidden around the set. The smoke machines continued to fill the air with a heavy mist to create atmosphere. The women at the tables were screaming hysterically. There was a lot to think about. What do I do? Why was he not running towards me as we'd painfully practised for days? I decided to take the initiative. The show must go on.

In my confusion, I calculated that I wouldn't be able to lift him without his jump and the leverage I gained from crouching on the floor, so I did what I knew best—tackle. I'd played many seasons of rugby league, and it seemed natural to take him out with a head-on tackle. I sprinted across to the door and hit him, lifting his body off the ground and then driving him with surprising and unexpected control on to the concrete floor. That signalled the end of the scene, so we sat around for a time until the director viewed the film. He returned to the set after a short time and said it was great and there was no need to do a second take. Was I relieved? Yes; I had survived.

Out came the drinks and the celebrations began. I searched for my final victim, who'd suffered more than any of us on the set, but I couldn't find him anywhere. Finally, I found someone who spoke English and knew where he was. I didn't want to believe what he said: "He's gone off to hospital. We think he's broken a wrist." Poor guy! After the celebrations, I received my hard-earned reward, 1,100 deutschmarks or 500 dollars US.

Fassbinder's energy was legendary and obvious on the set of Lilli Marlene. I recall a time when my presence was not required on set, and I sat down at one of the tables while the cameras filmed Lilli Marlene on stage. My pointy-toed shoes were killing me, so I unobtrusively slipped them off my feet under the table. I take a size thirteen, but the wardrobe department could only supply me with size eleven. I told the wardrobe people that I couldn't wear them, but after a few minutes of muffled conversation, I was told that if I didn't wear them, I'd be relegated to the status of an extra. I would lose my exalted position as an actor and suffer a large cut in pay. My immediate response was, "I'll wear them."

I did wear them, and it was torture, especially with the action and movement my part required. Every possible moment, I took them off my feet and snatched a few moments of luxurious relief. This was one of those moments. Suddenly, as I revelled in my indulgence, Fassbinder fixed his eyes on me and gave an order in German. I had no idea what he said. It came again and again, every time louder than the previous command. I glanced around helplessly until someone said in English, "He's telling you to put your shoes on."

I quickly inserted my feet into the size elevens, but he broke into uncontrolled sobbing. His crew tried to console him, but their efforts failed. A crewmember led him to the back of the set to regain his composure. Half an hour passed before he reappeared and continued directing the film. Fassbinder was a highly-strung guy, but reputed to be one of the best directors in Europe at the time.

1,100 deutschmarks was a small fortune. I'd survived for six months on a tight budget of twenty dollars a day. Now I was rich. So for my final three weeks in Europe, instead of hitchhiking, I bought a first class rail pass and experienced the luxury of sleeping on board a train. Three grand meals at restaurants every day replaced cooking for myself, and skimpy meals of bread and cheese. I travelled through Portugal and took an overnight train to Paris. My final days were spent in high living and magnificent touring.

Chapter Nineteen - A Brush with Death

"All men should strive
to learn before they die
what they are running from, and to, and why."
James Thurber

On my final day in Munich, 26th September, I walked into the Oktoberfest venue and celebrated with a few steins for most of the afternoon, accompanied by loud and boisterous music. Friendly drinkers from just about every nation on earth celebrated around me. German men and women in their traditional dress talked and laughed in small groups around long tables. Others clapped and danced to bright music churned out by musicians scattered throughout the huge marquees. Young German women with generous cleavage served overflowing steins to grateful patrons, and the distinctive aroma of German sausage mingled with beer wafted through the crowds. I breathed in the relaxed, joyful atmosphere. This is what I'd dreamed it might be. But things were about to change.

Around nine o'clock in the evening, my stomach announced it needed attention. I searched for something to fill the void. I'd been so caught up in the festive atmosphere that I'd not eaten for hours. Whole cooked chickens were selling from a nearby stall, so I reached into my money belt for a few deutschmarks.

It didn't take me long to consume that chook, then I continued wandering for an hour or more, soaking up the festivities. Slowly, I headed for the main gate to exit the grounds and take a bus back to my accommodation. Near the gate, a vendor was selling German sausages, one of my favourites with a spectacular flavour, possibly pork. I lined up in the queue, thinking to myself, *I don't need this. I've had a chicken an hour ago and I'm full.*

I waited, but the queue progressed slowly. I almost stepped out of line to move on, but the irresistible aroma of hot sausage kept me in place. I was almost at the counter when a deafening explosion rocked the place. Everyone stopped and stared toward the main gate, the source of the blast. It sounded as if a huge gas bottle had exploded. Screams and sounds of pandemonium came from outside the entrance. Sirens of emergency vehicles pierced the air. Whatever it was, it was major. After a minute or so, people cautiously resumed what they'd been doing. I paid for my unnecessary sausage, and ten minutes later exited through the main gate towards the bus stop. The screams and sirens were now silent.

Outside the gate, I walked into a scene I'll never forget. Chaos. A bomb had ripped through the area. It was a terrible sight. Blood, glass and debris covered the road. Onlookers walked past dazed. My stomach churned, and I stood rigid, frozen by the devastation. I couldn't see any trace of the parked ambulances that I'd noticed when entering the gate earlier. I assumed that since they were in the right place at the right time, they'd been prepared for any emergency. I was staggered at the speed of the removal of the victims' bodies. German efficiency! To one side stood a horse and decorated cart used to transport tourists around the grounds. The horse stood silently, not moving a muscle, blood flowing from wounds, small pieces of steel embedded in its body. I walked on, leaving the devastation and thinking that if I'd not stopped to buy that sausage, I might have been dead or badly injured. Strangely, my greed had saved me. Gluttony was good.

Later, I learnt that thirteen people died instantly, including three German children, and over 200 suffered terrible injuries. It was the worst act of terrorism on West German soil since World War II. Gundolf Kohler, a geology student, was responsible and died in the explosion. He had placed the bomb in a litterbin, and the blast had devastated an area the size of a soccer field. The bomb, made from a British mortar projectile, had been modified to ensure intense fragmentation would increase deaths and injuries. Kohler was reported to be a right-winged extremist, and suspicions remain about whether he acted alone.

Armed with my hard-earned dollars from a brief acting career, I bought a first-class Euro Rail pass and explored Spain, Portugal, Madrid, Paris, France, Switzerland, Austria, and Italy. I could not resist a return visit to the US, where I travelled the West Coast, and arrived back in Australia with fifty dollars in my pocket.

* * *

It's a great experience to go away, and it is a great feeling to return home. I count myself most fortunate to be so rich, having my roots firmly grounded in two cultures. But isn't that true of most Australians? We are a multicultural mix with our origins either in the United Kingdom, Europe, Middle East, Asia, and the Americas. We have made our way Down Under from diverse cultures and climates. Only our indigenous people can claim pure pedigree.

I respect our aboriginal people and their relationship with the land. It saddens me to see continuing discrimination against particular nationalities that have found their way to our shores, many who, like my father, were escaping the oppression and brutality of authoritarian regimes. I wonder how my father's life would have been different if he had not suffered the greed and deceit of others in his early days in Nowra. What difference it may have made for us as a family if we'd not been shunned, discriminated against and called 'wogs'.

However, we cannot change the past. We cannot change people. We can only change how we respond, and that's what Dad did. That's what we did as a family. We survived and found a way, even though Dad never felt fully part of Australian culture. He secretly longed for the embrace of his land and his people.

My journey heightened awareness of our young history as a nation. We have never been an occupied people, unlike the tribes of Europe. We rest on the false security of the Pacific and Atlantic moat that separates us from our European brothers, but as Edmund Burke said, *Slavery is a weed that grows in every soil. We should never take our freedom for granted.*

I landed at Sydney airport, and John drove me home. He drove and I talked. My thoughts went to Dad. How would he respond to me? What would he say? I'd spent many years trying to gain his approval and was desperate to hear him say he was proud of me. My main motivation to visit Latvia was an attempt to gain his respect. Geographic distance created emotional distance, and combined with his severe attitude, we'd grown apart. As John and I drew closer to home, I wondered what kind of welcome I'd receive from Dad.

It was a quiet homecoming. Mum approached me with open arms. "It's so good to see you, Peter," she said as she enveloped me in a hug.

I sat and talked with Mum and Dad at the kitchen table. Dad seemed genuinely pleased to see me. He listened intently as I related my visit with his mother and brother, and drank in every detail of my visit to Riga. His eyes moistened when I mentioned I'd left money for Uncle John in an envelope. Dad understood how much that would mean to his brother. I said nothing about my desire to take him Riga. The dust from my adventure needed to settle before that subject was put on the table. I was unsure if our relationship would survive, travelling together, especially with the added stress of maintaining a low profile in occupied territory.

* * *

I bought a place in Hockey's Lane at Cambewarra — a bold move with the little money I possessed, but I believed I could manage the repairs. I picked Dad up after work to show him my pride and joy. He surveyed the place for a few minutes, then said, "You've got a lot of work to do here." Not one hint of celebration. And he gave only one piece of advice: "Plant fruit trees and nuts."

A return trip to Latvia never left my mind. In the weeks and months that followed, I kept a watchful eye on the world stage. America called to me, and I responded with a three-month tour in 1983. The thirst developed from my earlier visit, and I immersed myself in the bustling cities, quiet towns, and unending countryside.

I saw the Lilli Marlene movie in New York at a cinema holding a festival of Fassbinder movies. After paying my money, I settled back to watch the action. I enjoyed the movie, finding the story stimulating and exciting. When my fight scene came on, for a fleeting moment my whole face covered the screen, and I wanted to say to the stranger in the seat behind me, "That's me."

I was surprised at how short the fight scene was in its final form — I guess no more than a minute. It had taken us three days to practise and prepare for it! Amazing. Later, I read about Fassbinder's tragic death at only thirty-seven years old, from a lethal cocktail of cocaine and barbiturates. One of the most influential figures in the New German Cinema, his work was intentionally provocative and designed to disturb. He'd kept a frenetic pace in filmmaking. In fewer than fifteen years he'd completed forty feature-length films, plus television film series, three short films, video productions, twenty-four stage plays and radio plays. This incredible and talented bloke often acted in his own productions and in others' films and theatre. He was also an author, cameraman, composer, designer, editor, producer and theatre manager. I'd experienced first-hand his incredible creative energy when working on the set.

My grandmother's death in 1984 brought great grief to our family. The sad news came in a letter from Uncle John. Dad read the letter and then quietly retreated to his garage. He needed to grieve alone. Over the following months, he withdrew into himself, and I knew his mind was in distant Riga. Guilt weighed heavily as I thought of the special time I'd had with his mother, my grandmother. Dad would've given anything to have seen her before she died, but he'd missed out. I was embarrassed to raise the subject with him and resolved that one day I would help him make the healing visit to his family and his homeland. Also, the poverty of Uncle John and my grandmother weighed heavily. They needed our help — more than the few shoes we sent occasionally — and I vowed to make it happen. That day would come, and with it more drama and danger than I'd ever imagined. However, before my return adventure, a chance meeting changed my life.

Part 2

Chapter Twenty - The Girl at the Counter

"I learned this, at least, by my experiment: that if one advances confidently in the direction of his dreams, and endeavours to live the life which he has imagined, he will meet with a success unexpected in common hours."
Henry David Thoreau, Walden.

I stood at the map counter where I worked at Shoalhaven Council when an attractive young woman entered, looking for 100 map hangers. She'd only recently joined the Soil Conservation Service and had been given the task of setting up the maps in their office. She had ordered the required number but wanted to be proactive and came to council in an attempt to obtain enough to commence the job.

"I'll see what I can find for you," I offered enthusiastically.

I checked our stores and, to her great disappointment and mine, found only a few available. But, out to impress, I was keen to help. First, I went to the Engineers' Department. They had around forty hangers. Next stop was Health and Building. I removed all that remained of their supply from their drawers. After that, I visited Town Planning, where I dived into the confidential drawers containing plans for future developments in the region.

"What are you doing?" one of the workers asked as I searched through the cabinets.

"I need map hangers, but I don't have time to explain fully now because it's urgent," I replied. I gathered what I could from there, then continued to run from department to department, collecting as many of these precious items as possible. I returned to the counter and gave them to the young woman.

She smiled at me. "Thank you so much. You're amazing. I hope it wasn't too much trouble."

"No" I replied, my heart racing. "It was easy."

"My name's Margie."

"I'm Peter, and I'm an engineer."

After regaining my composure, my thoughts went to the bloke in the Town Planning Department who might possibly report me to his boss. In my haste to impress Margie, I'd been abrupt and recognised that I'd upset him. That might mean trouble for me. It'd be good insurance to have Margie as my backup, so if my boss queried me, I'd give him Margie's telephone number and tell him to ring her up so she could verify my story.

So I took a deep breath and asked, "May I have your telephone number, please?"

"I'm not that easy," came her quick response. "You're going to have to work harder than that."

My face blushed, and I thought, *You're different.* But I didn't have her telephone number — very frustrating! That encounter created an internal chemical reaction that simmered for months.

I met Margie a second time at a party one of the young women in the council had organised. I picked up on the grapevine that Margie would be there, and on the strength of this information, I managed to find her number and phoned to see if she wanted a lift.

I dialled the number with my heart in my mouth, and I had to take a sip of water to relieve the dryness in my throat.

"Hello, this is Margie."

"Hi. It's Peter from the council. I was the one who helped you with the map hangers. I hope you don't mind me phoning, but I understand you're going to a party next Saturday night, and I wondered if you'd like a lift?"

"I remember you, Peter."

My heart raced in the silence as she considered my offer. I desperately wanted to hear a 'yes'.

"That's very kind of you," she said finally. "Yes, I'd love to go with you."

My heart sang. I could have leapt over the moon. The following Saturday evening, I picked her up at the appointed time and set out for the party venue. On the way, she told me about her family and her impressive brothers. Suddenly, around the halfway mark from Nowra to Huskisson, the car in front of us collided with a kangaroo. We saw it as it happened. The driver pulled off the road, and I followed and stopped behind him. The front guard of his car had been pushed against the wheel. Margie had just been telling me about her extraordinary brothers and how strong they were, and I thought this was my big opportunity to make an impression. So I took hold of the damaged guard, gave it a huge wrench and pulled it off the car. The driver stared at me, stunned and unimpressed. He mumbled something about there being more damage now compared to the original damage done by the kangaroo. The kangaroo sat by the roadside, stunned. It appeared to have a broken hip.

Margie asked the driver, "What are you going to do about the kangaroo?"

The guy replied, "I'm not going to do anything."

"Well, you just can't leave it there, that's cruel." Margie turned to me. "Peter, have you got a tyre lever or a bar?"

I produced one from the boot of my car and handed it to the driver.

The guy recoiled. "Don't give it to me."

"Give it to me," Margie said impatiently. She grabbed the tyre lever off me, went across to the kangaroo and gave it three solid whacks across the head.

Wow, this is some woman. I couldn't watch, but the kangaroo was now out of its misery.

And I was hooked. A day never went by without me thinking about Margie Campbell.

A short time later, Margie organised birthday drinks at the local pub and, wanting to surprise her, I secretly ordered a birthday cake. The candle-lit cake appeared on the night with accompanying song and cheering from friends and workmates. When Margie eventually discovered who'd provided the cake, she said, "Really, I hardly know him!"

* * *

When I gave Dad the news that his brother had never received any of the shoes we'd sent, Dad became angry and frustrated, even though he understood that this was common Soviet practice — corruption was an integral part of border control and society in general. Dad decided to try again, but this time he sent just one shoe. A few weeks later, Dad met me with a smile, waving a letter from his brother and saying, "He got it. He got it." The following day, he sent the remaining shoe. We now had proof that the system could be beaten. This gave me hope and I continued to think about taking Dad to Riga.

I'd developed some of Dad's cunning, an essential skill if you're thinking of hitchhiking around the world and sneaking into Latvia. Craftiness is essential if you're to outwit the Soviets, a critical challenge for my return visit.

My position in the council provided me with increasing responsibility and developed my confidence in the face of difficulties.

It was great preparation for helping Dad achieve his dream of a return to Riga. As it turned out, I required far more cunning in managing the Soviet system than I had previously.

My new boss was rarely on-site. It fell on me to take the lead, which I didn't mind. On one occasion, we had a job to install water mains along a rural road, and I noticed the guys were not working anywhere near their capacity. With the boss hardly ever around, I needed to find a way to motivate them. If I chastised them, they'd only complain, and it'd make them even more resistant. This job entailed installing 100 millimetre pipeline. Usually, we laid 150 metres in a day, but I believed more was possible. My diary told me we had twenty-five days until Easter. I had enough money for twenty-eight days, so I thought that if these guys could finish in twenty-five days, I'd be ahead. I called a meeting of the work team and said:

"There's a new policy at the council called the Incentive Policy. If you finish this job before Easter, you'll get the remaining days off on full pay. The hours you work will go on your time sheet as usual, and I'll sign them off. I have the authority to do it."

My frustration made me willing to experiment with just about any innovation. I wanted to get the job done. I was putting my job on the line, but I thought it was worth a try. They'd be paid for the work; they'd do the job well; the work would be complete, and everyone would win. So the guys had a meeting. Two of the workmen were union reps, and I wondered how they would respond. After a short while, the men came back and said they were willing to give it a go as a trial.

I told them that they could work any hours they liked. Historically, work was often slow in the mornings because it took the teams some time to get into the rhythm. I floated the suggestion that the backhoe operator might start early and dig the trench, so that when the rest of the guys arrived later, they could lay the pipes. I suggested that the new apprentice, who'd just started work with us, could take over the backhoe operator's job when he left at three o'clock. Some hands-on experience for the apprentice in doing the backfilling would give him good experience.

"You don't have to do any of this," I said. "They're only suggestions you might want to consider."

The following day I turned up around lunchtime and discovered that they'd already completed the usual day's work of laying 150 metres of pipe. I was thrilled that my plan would work and figured that the council would be pleased to have the job completed ahead of schedule. The following days, the pace increased further. Everyone was happy. The team was motivated, and no one complained. They worked together as a team, cooperatively and in good spirits. Also, the guys didn't take any days off, so I thought the approach had great potential.

One night, the highly motivated backhoe operator struggled with sleep. At three o'clock in the morning, he decided to go to the worksite and begin digging the trench. So our backhoe operator started his work in the pitch black of night. This wasn't a problem because the area contained few houses, and they were some distance from the road. Also the backhoe had lights fitted for emergency night work, which made an early start possible. However, at five o'clock in the morning, he was digging outside the only house close to the road—an old fibro house, set back about seven metres. The noise and flashing lights woke the owner, who put on his dressing-gown and asked the backhoe operator what was going on.

"I'm digging a trench for the water mains," he replied.

"I know that, but it's five o'clock in the morning. What are you doing here now?"

"I've been digging since four o'clock."

"Who do you work for?" he asked in disbelief.

"Shoalhaven Council."

"You work for the council, and you're on-the-job at four o'clock in the morning?"

"Yes, Peter Jirgens, our boss, said we can work any hours we like."

At that point, the homeowner called me.

"Do you know your workman is here, right now, working? What's going on?"

"Really. I didn't know he'd started early."

"It's dark."

"I know. I'm surprised too," I replied.

"You work for the council?" he asked.

"Yes, I do."

"I don't believe this. Why is he here now?"

"I don't know, but I do know the boys are keen to get the job completed before Easter. I don't know why he's there at the moment, but I don't want to stop him because he seems keen. Would you mind telling him to go 100 metres further down the road away from your place? He can come back and complete the section outside your house after seven o'clock."

"I don't really care. I just can't believe this is a council job."

I employed that approach for the following twenty-five years while I worked in the council. I only did it when it was important to knock the job over to save inconvenience to businesses and the public.

Chapter Twenty-One - Pushing the Boundary

"Do not go where the path may lead, go instead where there is no path and leave a trail."
Ralph Waldo Emerson

Another challenge was laying a sewer pipe under the new bridge at Nowra. The council intended to put it to tender, but I said I thought the council could manage it. It would be tricky, requiring us to work off barges with ropes and pulleys, and the movement of the tide and the strength of the current needed to be considered. It would take some skill and effort to put the heavy pipes into place. The challenge required setting up ropes and pulleys to haul the pipes into place from a barge floating on the river and secure them with brackets under the bridge. Manoeuvring the pipes accurately with the changing river height—due to tides and wave action caused by wind—would be tricky. We started the job, and my blokes, who were used to working in trenches, now found themselves working on the river. The conditions were pleasant, especially when they could fish at lunchtime. However, the job slowed, and I became concerned. We were only completing two pipes a day, so I said to the team:

"If you can manage four pipes a day, you can have half a day off on pay when the job is completed."

One problem I faced on any job, and particularly that one, was the hire of machinery. The gear we used was expensive. Completing the job in the least possible time saved a huge amount. From that point on, the guys installed four pipes a day and some worked through their lunch hour and for an hour or so after work.

The day I retired from the council, many councillors were present, including the mayor, deputy mayor and many of my colleagues. I said during my farewell speech:

"I've got a confession to make. I introduced a policy twenty-five years ago which has not yet been ratified by the council."

I told a few of the stories of what we'd been doing over the years and how I successfully conducted my work like a business.

After I left the council, a memo circulated, banning this type of practice. It said: "Under no circumstances is this practice ever to happen again."

I knew it was illegal, but over the years I possibly saved the council hundreds of thousands of dollars. It was about risk management, ensuring the workplace was always as safe as possible. I had the challenge of taking risks that I believed could benefit my team and the council, but also ensuring it was a safe workplace and good standards of safety were maintained. I think I took greater risks after I left the council, particularly when I started doing airport runways, something I knew nothing about, but that's another story.

Building a water pipe across the Crookhaven River created a further challenge at the council. It measured 700 feet long and had to lie in a trench on the riverbed, and I was the only one in the work team who could swim. We built a railway line through a farmer's field to transport the pipes to the edge of the river, then we had to weld the pipes together and dig a trench across the river, which was only two meters deep at that point. We mounted a backhoe on a pontoon, and to secure it, I drove five-metre stakes into the riverbed every five metres. The only way I could hammer the stakes into position was with a sledge-hammer while standing on the back of a dinghy. Because I was the only swimmer, it was my job. I set out with a large sledge-hammer in a little aluminium dinghy with a five horsepower motor attached to drive these stakes into place. It was tricky, standing in the dinghy, swinging the sledge-hammer accurately onto the top of the stake. Occasionally, I missed, and since I couldn't let the sledge-hammer go, I had to go with it, over the side of the dinghy into the river. Then I threw the sledge-hammer back into the dinghy, clambered over the side and continued driving the stake into place. Once the stakes were set, we tied the pontoon containing the backhoe to it and then dug the trench.

When the tide was right and there was no movement in the river, we tied a series of forty-four gallon drums to the pipeline. Then, with the help of a crane, we moved the pipeline into place above the trench. Next, we pumped water into the pipe and cut the drums free. The pipe slowly sank into the trench, but around seven or eight drums remained attached to the pipe, which was now lying in two metres of water. As the only one who could swim, I got the job of diving into the cold water with a pair of tin-snips to cut each drum free. Holding myself down was an effort by itself, and I still had to find the ties in the murky water and cut the wire. Once the drum was free, it rocketed to the surface, shooting well above the water level, then descended with a thump onto the surface of the water. I had to be careful not to return to the surface too quickly after I cut the tie, otherwise I'd have a forty-four gallon drum crushing my cranium. My lung capacity increased about twenty-five percent by the time I finished releasing those drums. This ability and my aerobic fitness from sport helped save my life in a brush with death in 1986. I loved these challenging and interesting jobs.

Possibly the riskiest project occurred when I was the Northern Regional Engineer, responsible for maintaining the roads and facilities in my region. I regularly presented reports to the council, setting priorities for reconstruction and resealing. The factors I had to consider included traffic flow determined from road counters, businesses, gradient, tourist attractions and schools. One day, a large allocation of funding appeared for a particular road that had been elevated from five on the priority list to number one. My enquiries proved fruitless to its sudden rise to top priority. Having no alternative, I went out with our surveyor and began marking out the survey pegs to determine the profile. Residents from streets higher on the priority list noticed the survey pegs and phoned me to find out why their street had been suddenly reprioritised. The road ranking information was made public to all residents so everybody was able to see where their street ranked and when it was likely to be attended to. Without any explanation from the council, I was left with the task of inventing reasons as to why the reprioritisation had taken place. I found it embarrassing and awkward to have to field angry calls from residents who believed the council was railroading them.

Then I discovered that a senior member of council had recently bought a home in the street in question. This person exercised considerable power in the council. His new purchase was half a kilometre from the end of the sealed section of his road. I was furious when I discovered this information and was determined to seal the road up to the start of his driveway. That would expose what he had done. I believed I couldn't be sacked unless I'd done something corrupt, but promotions would now be impossible to achieve. And that's what I did. Money had been allocated to ensure the bitumen would reach well beyond the new home, but I carefully calculated the costing for the project to ensure the road would be sealed up to, but not including, his driveway. Road construction requires that priority be given to drainage, and I used the money for drainage well past his property, leaving only enough funds to seal the gravel road to his driveway. I took photographs of what I was doing, and made sure I ticked all the boxes.

Some days later, after the road was sealed, I was driving back with work colleagues in a council car when a senior staff member called me on the two-way radio and said, "Call me now."

"I'll be back in the office in about twenty minutes," I replied.

"Call me now," he growled.

We stopped the car in the little town of Wandandian, and I phoned him from a telephone box.

"Why did you only seal the road up to the driveway?" he asked.

"Nobody told me he lived there," I replied innocently.

"Don't you know where he lives?" came the angry response.

"I believe he lives in south of Nowra." Which he did, as he'd not moved into his new home.

"Seal the road up to half a kilometre beyond the house tomorrow."

"There's no money left in the budget."

"Don't worry about the budget, just get it done."

I took my team to the worksite the following morning to complete the job, but it was raining. It rained for three weeks. During that time, the newspapers got hold of the story, and it became front page news. A former State Parliamentarian, but still active in the electorate, made an issue of it, which further embarrassed the person. Allegations of corruption and threats of legal action followed. Soon after, I was told that 'he was out to get me', so I had to act with great caution.

Somehow, I managed to meet the challenge of following projects and managed to hold my position. Over time, I achieved the reputation of conquering the tricky jobs. If any projects needed careful scrutiny because of overhead power lines or blasting rock faces in difficult locations, or had rush jobs with limited completion dates, I managed to land the assignment. I liked a challenge and my superiors knew it. I also hated people abusing power and innocent people suffering.

A stupid tension existed between the indoor and outdoor

staff at the council. I think it was my experience as a rugby league and cricket player that gave me an understanding of managing a team in the workplace. I believe every member of the team is important and necessary for success, and that nobody is more important than anyone else. I had a team of low-paid labourers who did the backbreaking work on the roads and sewerage projects. They were a great team and each of them as good as any man on the council. At Christmas, I took up a collection from contractors and provided a party for them and their families at my home. The total amount collected was $1,500 and covered meat, beer and drinks for the kids. Each family brought a salad. The collection was an illegal activity and it might have cost me my job, but I was willing to take the risk. I never favoured any of the contractors with work. In my own mind, I believed I was ethical and fair. My concern was for those who were looked down on and discriminated against.

Chapter Twenty-Two - Mixed Emotions

*"Our chief want is someone who will inspire us
to be what we know we could be."*
Ralph Waldo Emerson

Late in 1985, Dad opened the letter Mum had taken from the letterbox earlier that afternoon. What he read in that letter transformed his dream into a reality. "John says that the Russians are softening their controls, and it's possible for me to go to Riga."

Stunned, Mum turned from the sink where she was rinsing a cup. "Let's not rush into this. Please take time to think about it," she pleaded.

I took a few deep breaths to control my excitement. Dad's eyes lit up as he looked at me, and I sensed that he'd already made his decision. We'd been watching the dramas between the USA and Russia unfold on the international stage. President Reagan and Gorbachev were struggling to find agreement to end the nuclear arms build-up. Both had pressures from within their countries to end the Cold War, and the Russian economy was sagging under massive military expenditures. To receive a letter from Uncle was a great leap forward.

This development took me by surprise and created a real dilemma. I was playing the best football of my life. Until I turned twenty, I struggled to get into a footy team. I played with my mates at Nowra and ended up most weeks sitting on the bench as a reserve. I usually joined the team for half a game, never a full match. My engineering studies in Wollongong interrupted my training, meaning that I couldn't play with Nowra, so I introduced myself to the coach of the Berry team. The coach placed me in the front row of first grade. Unbelievable! Four weeks later, we played my old team, Nowra Warriors. They were leading the competition and Berry was coming last. On that unforgettable day, the sun had broken through heavy clouds, bringing warmth to counter the icy breeze. I walked out onto the wet field at Berry and spotted Dad in the crowd. I took a deep breath and glanced back again. No, I wasn't mistaken; it was him! My reaction was similar to when he appeared at my cricket grand final. Filled with pride, I put my head down and played like I'd never played before. I had something to prove to him. Three tries were recorded against my name during the game, and I was named Man of the Match.

A year later, I found myself selected to play the touring British Test team, who were unbeaten in Australia. The coach selected me over a Group Seven player, and consequently, rumblings were heard around the region. So I stepped up my training, ready to put my best foot forward. On a Wednesday night in Sydney, our Southern Division team ran onto the field to face the British and waited for the whistle to blow. Suddenly, a chant erupted from the grandstand: "Jirgo, Jirgo."

What? Who was calling my name? I searched the crowd and my heart leapt. My teammates from first grade and half the Nowra Warriors had hired a coach and driven to Sydney to watch me play. Tears ran down my face as the referee signalled the start of the match. I was determined from that moment to play my best, and my performance shot up a couple of levels. We kicked off, and instantly the British forward who caught the ball was in my sights. He was huge compared to our boys, but I took him out and was penalised for an over-vigorous tackle. First tackle of the game and first penalty! The ball was kicked out, with the British completing five more phases of play until I found myself bringing down another forward with a solid tackle. A second tackle and a second penalty, quickly followed by another lethal tackle and a further penalty. Three penalties were given against me in the opening minutes of the game; I was on fire. The crowd went wild. The referee came over to me and repeated, "Settle down, settle down. I don't want to send you off."

I did settle down, and combined with a mate from the northern region to amass eighty tackles between us — he made forty-two, and me, thirty-eight. Again, I was named Man of the Match. It's amazing what encouragement can do. You can achieve things you never thought possible.

I played in the Country Firsts in 1977, and in one game I had to mark Arty Beetson, who was captain of the Australian team at the time. He was my hero, one of the best forwards of his time. The coach asked me to mark him and told me I had to take him out. All I thought of was, *if only I could get his autograph.*

These and other performances contributed to the offer of football contracts from Sydney clubs. I earned more money from football than I received from my work with the council. Coaches I respected encouraged me to take the step into the big time. "You'll only get one chance at this, so take it," became the chorus of encouragement from the side lines. I couldn't put the decision off. Clubs needed to finalise their teams. In one way, it was one of the hardest decisions I have made. I'd invested much pain and hard work over many years to reach elite level. Was I prepared to throw it all away? A decision had to be made. I chose not to play football for the season. The opportunity to accompany Dad to his homeland, walk the streets of Riga, wander through the fields of his old farm became the priority.

Dad wrote to Uncle John and checked the current political status. The reply was cautious optimism. Though security was a little more relaxed, limitations were still in place. Latvians were restricted from travelling outside their place of residence. The threat of imprisonment or Soviet strong-arm tactics was still possible. However, my successful visit in 1980 gave me hope of a trouble-free return. Dad was sixty-four years old and the 'clock was ticking'. My relationship with him had improved, but his manner and my attitude still kept us a safe distance from each other.

Dad asked Uncle John what might be a good time to visit and whether he could bring anything they needed from Australia. Weeks later, a response came confirming the relaxation of Russian control and asking if we were able to bring a synthesizer. As far as Uncle was aware, they did not exist in Latvia. Dad searched around Sydney and bought a second-hand instrument for around 500 dollars. Dad, being an accomplished musician, checked it out and it performed well, so we explored how much it would cost to take into Latvia. The import duty quoted at 1,200 US dollars in our thinking was extreme, but we decided to pay the amount. The synthesizer would mean so much to my cousin and his family. No bands in Latvia had such an instrument, and it would be a valuable asset for the community.

No real discussion took place about whether I would accompany Dad. It was an assumption that grew to reality as the days of preparation progressed. Mum chose not to fly and said she was happy to mind the house. She was a nervous traveller to the extent that she never wanted to hold a driver's licence. Dad took some comfort in the fact I knew the ropes. So he deferred to me for guidance and suggestions. He'd never been in an aircraft before, so this was his first flight. I felt affirmed knowing that he seemed to value my experience. He never said it in so many words, but I sensed it. Our relationship lost some of its distance, and we commenced to work together on our adventure.

When my sister Julie and her husband Michael chose to join the party, I decided to take extra leave from work and visit Asia for a few weeks. The challenge of walking the Annapurna Trail in the Himalayas had become more than a fascination. The 230 kilometre trail winds through the spectacular mountains of Central Nepal and contains Thorong La Pass, the highest pass in the world at 5,416 metres (17,769 feet). I had to do it.

Julie and Michael were happy to accompany Dad, and Dad was pleased with the arrangement. I would meet them in Bangkok. Flights were booked, visas finalised and travel arrangements put in place. I needed someone to look after my home and my beautiful dog Beau—the German shepherd pup that had emerged from the bush near my place after being abandoned by his mother. I'd raised him from a pup, and we were the best of mates.

A few days later, I met Margie at work. Our time together at the party had gone well. We'd enjoyed each other's company. Since then, I'd always been on the lookout for her when around the office. The few times I'd caught sight of her, she'd smiled and given me a wave. I'd returned the wave and said, 'Hi'. During these brief encounters, my heart had skipped a beat. My body told me she was definitely plugged into my radar. Margie came up to me in the lunchroom and said, "I hear on the grapevine that you're looking for a house-sitter?"

Those words lifted me off the ground. "Yes, I am. Are you looking for accommodation?"

The following week Margie moved her belongings into the second bedroom. She easily made friends with Beau, and being a country girl there was nothing she couldn't do around the house or the property. This was the perfect setup! I walked on air. Until I discovered that she was going out with one of the local boys. My world came crashing down. Devastating disappointment took hold of me for days. While she was only my house-sitter, I thought that move might have given me a foot in to the door of her heart. I tended to be shy around girls and waited to see if there was any interest before I declared my position. I liked Margie, more than I was willing to admit. She was something special, very special, and she seemed to like me, but now with the news of a competitor, I assumed her interest was nothing more than a casual friendship.

The more I thought about going away, the more anxious I became. My mind went viral: *She might be engaged by the time I return. How can I compete with this character when I'm on the other side of the world? Should I be open about my feelings for Margie now?* Here I was, poised, ready for an amazing adventure into Asia and then escorting Dad on a trip he'd dreamt of for decades, and I was torn down the middle. I thought about the adventure, my spirit rose. Then my mind went to Margie and this bloke, and my heart sank. The shine disappeared from my preparations.

A week before I was due to leave, my friends decided to give me a party. *That's nice*, I thought. It gave me a lift until I discovered Margie's new companion was the one organising it! He was throwing me a party because he was glad to see me go. The moment I received that information, my heart sank; I felt wretched, helpless and thought, *What hope have I got with Margie? While I'm away, this character will most likely be sitting in my lounge room with her! They'll be watching my* TV *together!* There was nothing I could do about it.

In the days that followed, my thinking changed a little. *While Margie was in my house, even if he was there, Margie would be reminded of my presence. Everywhere she looked in my home, she would, hopefully, see my ghost. I took hold of that thought.* It was all I had, and it gave me hope.

Chapter Twenty-Three - Kathmandu

"We travel, initially, to lose ourselves; and we travel, next, to find ourselves. We travel to open our hearts and eyes and learn more about the world than our newspapers will accommodate. We travel to bring what little we can, in our ignorance and knowledge, to those parts of the globe whose riches are differently dispersed. And we travel, in essence, to become young fools again—to slow time down and get taken in, and fall in love once more."
Pico Iyer

1986 was a memorable year. Top Gun and Crocodile Dundee hit the big screens; Billy Joel released *New York State of Mind*; Mike Tyson became the youngest heavyweight fighter in history; Bob Hawke was Prime Minister of Australia; Spain and Portugal joined the EEC; the Space Shuttle Challenger disintegrated, killing all on board; the Soviet Nuclear reactor at Chernobyl exploded on 26th April, and a breakthrough in US–USSR arms talks between Reagan and Gorbachev led to a commitment to disarm nuclear weapons. The latter signalled hope for Dad to return to Latvia. It was like two massive plates in the earth, which had ground against each other for decades, threatening destruction, had finally relented and relaxed. The relaxation provided space, a path that led to Latvia.

The day in March finally came when I boarded the plane at Sydney airport, knowing everything was set in place for our family visit to Riga. Every detail had been attended to. However, no matter how well plans are made, when the Soviet government is factored in, things can come unstuck, as we were soon to find out.

For three days, I dodged pedestrian, bikes, trucks, crowded buses, cars, and Tut Tuts in Bangkok. I believe the rules were 'there are no rules'. Though it felt dangerous to me, everyone appeared to survive the chaos. It was their way of life. I hired a motorbike, rode to Chang Mai and on through the mountains for a week, excited by my first taste of glittering monasteries set in green forests beneath towering mountains.

Back in Bangkok, the sun was well above the horizon when I walked onto the tarmac to board the DC3 for Kathmandu. It felt as if I were going on an Army manoeuver, walking up the ramp at the rear of the aircraft. The flight was uneventful until we came to the final part of the journey. Clouds hung over the mountains like huge balls of cotton wool, but there was no softness about these reservoirs of devastation. The captain announced that everyone was to remain seated. The cabin crew strapped themselves in, and minutes later the plane lurched violently and dropped twenty metres. A woman screamed behind me. My stomach asked me if I'd completed a somersault. The clouds swallowed up the mountains, and strong winds buffeted the plane. Two women in traditional Tibetan dress sitting opposite me appeared calm, and I wondered if such turbulence was typical for flights in this part of the world. The mature-aged couple seated in front of the women, however, had white faces and knuckles where they gripped the side of their seats.

Momentary glimpses of the runway appeared through the thick clouds. A flash of green terraced mountains disappeared as the aircraft rocked dangerously. One of the overhead lockers sprung open, two rows in front of my seat, and luggage crashed into the passageway. More screams sounded from the rear of the plane as the nose tilted forward along with the familiar clunk of the landing wheels locking into position.

My heart raced as we descended. I recalled the fierce electrical storm on my flight into Moscow when the plane had almost fallen out of the sky. That was nothing compared to this nightmare. I couldn't understand how the pilot believed it possible to land the aircraft with the fierce, unpredictable crosswinds. The plane dropped lower in the sky as the winds wrenched the plane sideways. I sat in the aisle seat and looked out of the cabin window on my right at the runway, two or three kilometres away. The next moment, the wind wrenched the plane in the opposite direction, and I could see the runway through the cabin window on my left. Moments later, the wind eased a little as the pilot wrestled to line the aircraft up with the airstrip. You could cut the tension in the air with a knife. The pilot gave no instruction to assume the crash position, but one older man, a few seats in front of me, took up the brace position. As the tarmac raced up to meet us, not a word was spoken: no screams, just silence. I was aware I was holding my breath, as I suspect everyone was. The wheels hit the runway with a thump, thump and we bounced in our seats. Instantly, an enormous cheer went up from the passengers, and they continued to clap and cheer until the aircraft came to a halt minutes later.

When I stood in the terminal waiting for my bag to arrive, two Nepalese security men walked up to me and asked me to follow them. We entered a small room, no larger than a toilet. They beckoned for me to remove my backpack and jacket, then they patted me down and then indicated I should turn 360 degrees. As I did so, we kept bumping into each other; two security guards, me and a large backpack, all in a confined space—bizarre! The weirdest experience ever.

I took a bus from the airport to Kathmandu along a road

lined with hundreds of school children. I knew their smiling faces weren't meant to be a special welcome for me, and I asked a passenger, who I suspected was a local, why they were there.

"They've heard the king is coming from the airport and want to welcome him," she replied.

Later, I heard that the king didn't appear, so the children were returned to their classrooms after a three-hour wait.

The road from the airport was smooth and wound its way eventually to the king's palace, located on one of the highest points of Kathmandu. I learnt later that it was the only sealed road in the country and was especially laid for the king. Apparently, he's one of the wealthiest men in the world.

The kaleidoscope of colour, odours, flies, cars, buses, chaos, poverty, people and the vastness of Kathmandu overwhelmed me. It was like going back 200 years, but I loved it. The first street I walked along, I looked down at the footpath and saw what I thought looked like blood. My eyes followed the flow to its source a few metres away on the footpath where a butcher was cutting up a goat. The baker, his fresh loaves of bread spread out on a mat, crouched beside an old lady selling bunches of flowers. A horse and cart rattled past, and a boy led two goats along the side of the road. This place was raw and alive!

"Excuse me, mister," a boy's voice said.

I ignored it. People pushed their craft, produce, anything of value into my face, hoping for a sale.

"Excuse me, mister, your shoe is broken," said the same voice, this time more persistent.

My shoe was not broken. I'd purchased the joggers weeks before in preparation for the trip. I continued on.

"Mister, please look, your shoe is broken. I can fix it." The dark-haired Nepalese boy walking beside me pointed to my right sneaker.

I glanced down. It did have a split on the side. I was amazed, but then considered that my oversized feet probably placed too much stress on the sides of the sneaker. Maybe it was a result of the contortions inflicted on me by the nightmare flight I'd just survived. The young man appeared to be a nice guy, so I said, "You can fix it for me?"

"Yes, sir. Please sit over here." He pointed to the gutter.

So I sat on the edge of the gutter and removed my sneaker. He produced a small bag with needles, cloth and leather patches. Minutes later, my sneaker was back on my foot, professionally repaired. "How much do I owe you?"

"Two dollars, thank you. Where are you staying?"

I gave him the address.

"I know where that is," he said. "I can take you there."

I followed him through the bustling streets for twenty minutes until he pointed to my guesthouse. "Thanks. Where do you live?"

"It's only a short distance. Would you like to see it?"

"Okay." I followed him for a couple of minutes, and he led me to the side of an old building. He removed a wooden door, revealing an area measuring no more than a cubic metre. I stared in disbelief. He lived under a house! "Where are your parents?"

"They live on a farm in the mountains. No room for me, so I came to the city to find work. I go home every three weeks to visit them."

His name was Aadi, and he was seventeen years old. I was moved by his story and wanted to help. We arranged to meet the following day, and he showed me the sights of Kathmandu. He returned the following day and together we explored more of the city. I paid him for his excellent service as a tour guide. On the third day, I hired a motorbike, and we visited his family in the mountains. Every kilometre or so we drove past women with hammers, smashing up rocks the size of footballs on the side of the road. Men loaded the crushed rock onto a truck and delivered it to building sites where it was used in construction.

We arrived at the farm and were greeted by the boy's parents. Aadi introduced me to his younger brothers and sisters, who stood shyly at a distance. Their home, a mud straw dwelling, had colourful mats strewn across the floor and chooks everywhere, scratching for food. His father took my shoe measurements and disappeared around the back of the hut. I produced a gift of Chinese checkers, which kept the family busy until dal bhat was served. A number of other villagers gathered in the doorway and watched quietly as we ate the meal. I felt privileged to sit amongst Aadi's family while he interpreted my questions and answers to his parents. They are beautiful people.

Mid-afternoon, I suggested to Aadi that we needed to return to Kathmandu. His father disappeared for a moment and returned with a pair of sandals. The soles were made of recycled car tyres and the uppers, leather. They fitted perfectly, and I wore them for years.

We returned to Kathmandu, and I farewelled Aadi. He obviously enjoyed my company because he invited me to his wedding in two weeks. Sadly, I declined, but I promised I'd call after my return from my Annapurna trek.

Chapter Twenty-Four - The Trek

"We need the tonic of wildness ... At the same time that we are earnest to explore and learn all things, we require that all things be mysterious and unexplorable, that land and sea be indefinitely wild, unsurveyed and unfathomed by us because [they are] unfathomable. We can never have enough of nature."
Henry David Thoreau, Walden

The following day, I arrived at the bus stop to go to Pokhara to commence the trek. The bus arrived, bursting with bodies, maybe forty or fifty, some seated, some standing. The driver, obviously keen for my money, pointed to the roof. "You up on top."

I clambered onto the roof and sat beside the luggage with another unfortunate victim who didn't speak English. I think he was pleased to see me. Five minutes later, without warning, the bus roared off. I clung on as best I could. Sitting on the roof gave me an excellent view of the road ahead, but my teeth chattered as we flew over corrugations. I wondered if the driver was trying to save petrol by lightening his load, attempting to dislodge the two bodies clinging to the roof. He swerved, without slowing, around larger holes in the road, which resulted in me and my silent travelling companion being flung from side to side. If the anchoring of the rusty roof rack broke free, we'd be catapulted into the rocky terrain.

I spotted a road worker pushing a huge rock, a metre high and a metre in diameter, which had been chiselled into the shape of a roller. It must have weighed three quarters of a tonne. I saw no signs of steamrollers, bobcats, or any heavy machinery on the roads. All roadwork was completed by backbreaking human effort.

The bus climbed for a while, and the road narrowed. A sizeable drop appeared on my left. Car bodies and buses lay strewn in the gorges, but the driver, possessing no fear, sped on. My prayers were answered when we finally stopped. My hands, arms, whole body ached from the pounding it'd suffered avoiding injury and possible death. My clothes were filthy, covered in grey dust. I wasn't prepared to let go of the roof rack to take a drink from my water bottle, and as a result, my tongue stuck to the top of my mouth.

That was my steamy, high adrenalin three-hour trip to Pokhara.

The following day, I took a taxi, a land rover, to the start of the walk. Locals, chooks and a goat crowded into the old vehicle with me, and we set off up a dusty track. We climbed, twisted and turned at a speed that caused me, again, to grip my seat for stability. A dry riverbed appeared, and we plunged down the embankment, loose stones flying in all directions. Somehow, I survived another Nepalese trip.

A welcome lunch helped repair some of the damage and gave me strength to commence my walk to Chomrong, where I spent the night. Many hikers hired sherpas, but I decided to carry my own backpack, which contained a small tent, sleeping bag, pocketknife and string, underwear, plastic bags to cover my shoes, hand-knitted woollen gloves and food.

The two days that followed overflowed with an intoxicating mix of mud, wooden and stone villages, mule trains, snow-covered pinnacles, dense green forests, stunning blue skies and friendly locals. The trail climbed 1000 metres and then dropped into a valley for 500 metres, winding its way towards the highest point of the trail, Thorong Pass. The river, coloured green-grey from snow and sediment, rushed past down the steep mountain terrain and provided companionship for most of my journey.

The seduction of the hot springs of Tatopani overtook me, and I took a leisurely rest there, soaking up the sun and the healing properties of the warm water. A young couple lay in the water, embracing. I thought of Margie. How good it would be to have her here, relaxing with me. Was she still going out with that bloke? Margie was never far from my mind. I often tormented myself thinking about her and what was going on in her relationship with the generous party-giver.

I paid two dollars for accommodation and was ushered into a house and introduced to my hosts for the night. A small fire with mats scattered around the perimeter sat in the middle of the room, and above it, goats' meat hung from the rafters to smoke. Due to the lack of refrigeration, this was the accepted method of curing meat, but Westerners usually found it produced vomiting and diarrhoea, so I avoided eating it. That night, however, I suspended my resolution and attacked a large chunk of the questionable goat meat, rice and maize. I took confidence in chewing and swallowing a clove of garlic each day as a precaution against stomach problems. It tasted delicious, and the garlic must have worked, because I had no problems. From that day on, I consumed goat meat whenever it was available.

On the fourth day, with the cool air of the early morning caressing my face, I set my course to Kalopani and Jomson, where I would spend the night. This stretch of the trail contained a challenging section that commanded great respect. Trail walkers described it as dangerous and treacherous when shared with a mule train. Mule trains were a common sight on the trail. The lead mule wore a brightly woven, multi-coloured cloth around its forehead. A bell hung from its neck to warn walkers to clear the track. The look of fear on the faces of children who scrambled to safety when they heard the first sound of the bell said it all. A dozen mules or more, unbound, followed along the rocky trail. Huge bags of rice, wheat, maize, and other provisions strapped to their sides increased their width significantly. Once on the move, they stopped for no one. They bulldozed their progress without deviation.

I approached this section of the trail on the mountain pass near Pisang. The trail is cut out of the rock face by hand. Locals created the ancient trail, hundreds of years ago—an amazing and dangerous feat. The narrow track winds its way along the cliff face, a sheer drop to the river on the other side. Ten minutes into this dodgy section, walking cautiously over the uneven rock, I heard a sound that struck fear into me. I stopped and listened. I was not mistaken. Up ahead came the familiar sound of the mule bell. My heart sank. Searching for the widest section of the trail, I walked another ten metres and found a slight indentation in the rock wall where I could press my shoulder.

At first, I thought I'd place my back against the wall, but that left the front of my body exposed to the bulging bags. I'd take up less room with my shoulder jammed against the wall. I waited nervously, hearing them, though they were still out of sight. Eventually, the first mule came into view with its colourful cloth fixed to its head, straining under the weight of the heavy bags of rice strapped to its sides. The constant sound of the bell had served its purpose and cleared the road. I saw at least a dozen mules behind the leader, and the mule driver was still not in sight. He often walked behind the train to ensure the pace was maintained.

The lead mule approached, and I braced myself, pleased I'd not chosen to position myself on the other side of the track. With little space, a gentle bump from bag or beast would have pushed me over the edge to fall into the river or the rocks far below. The lead mule did not alter its speed, just walked on past, leaving a strong animal smell in its wake. I noted the beads of perspiration on its neck. The second mule passed, its bags narrowly missing me. My heart beat sped up, and I breathed heavily, but the third beast passed successfully. I soothed myself by thinking, *I'm going to make it.* There was something captivating, almost hypnotic, about their movement. The swaying and rhythm reassured me. I told myself to relax. It was going to be fine.

The sixth beast approached with its cargo of grain. It turned it head slightly to look at me as it passed. I'm not sure if that movement, as slight as it was, resulted in reducing the distance between itself and me. The hessian bag caught the lower corner of my backpack. The momentum spun me around so the bag of grain pressed into my stomach. I adjusted my feet quickly so as not to fall. Falling was not an option under the sharp hooves of a mule train. The train maintained its pace and rhythm, and I rolled along the wall. One second, my face and chest were pressed into the roughly chiselled rock wall. The next, I heard the lock on my backpack scraping along the unforgiving cliff face. I noticed blood on my hands. My heart raced, and I struggled to stay on my feet while I rolled, out of control, along the cliff face, crushed by the unrelenting power of the mules.

Eventually, I stood and watched the final animals and the driver disappear, the bell continuing to sound its warning to oncoming travellers. It was time to take stock. My hands were cut from the rough edges of the cliff wall. My chest was throbbing. Could I have broken ribs? Both legs were grazed and bruised from my desperate efforts to remain upright. I sat down and took a long drink from my flask. That was close, but I'd survived. It could have been worse. I wondered what would happen if an injury occurred that prevented me from walking. It was a long way to any medical help. I stood up and lifted the backpack onto my shoulders. Little did I know my scare with the mule train would pale into insignificance compared with what lay ahead.

For many kilometres, I walked behind an old man I imagined had been a porter his entire life. Hunched over, he balanced a six by six foot post, four metres long. A kit bag and an array of personal gear hung from the end of the beam in front of him. His feet were wider than they were long.

I came upon a team of local men completing construction of a bridge over the fast-flowing, milky-coloured river. The remains of the previous bridge were still visible. One of the crew spoke English, and he told me that they'd cut down trees within a twenty metre radius, then stacked the logs in place, on top of each other from each side of the river until they met in the middle. I understood it took about a month to complete the bridge. I marvelled at their ingenuity and daring.

The women on the trail amazed me with the mass of firewood they carried on their heads. Each village had been stripped of trees within a five-kilometre radius, forcing the women to go further to gather wood for their heating and cooking. Goats ate the shoots that would otherwise have formed the next generation of timber, which made it impossible for the landscape to recover, and the harsh weather also eroded huge areas. The firewood, neatly stacked on roofs, indicated the prosperity of the family. Stones secured the many rooves without firewood. Nails in this part of the world were non-existent.

I pressed on to Jomson and the Mustang region, which includes the world's deepest gorge of the Kali Gandaki River. The trail reaches an altitude of 3,800 metres or 12,464 feet. I continued along the Kali Gandaki River Gorge, gazing in awe at the amazing peaks of Annapurna-I and Dhaulagiri, both of which reach heights in excess of 8,000 metres or 26,240 feet. I passed monasteries hundreds of years old, caves, local tribes and scenic beauties of the varying landscapes, including the world's deepest gorge in the Kali Gandaki Region.

Muktinath was the launching place for the great challenge of my expedition, Thorong La, the highest navigable pass in the world. It's a graveyard for walkers who have been caught by freezing, unpredictable changes in the weather. None of the villages on the Annapurna Tail have electricity or phone coverage. Communication is by word of mouth. Muktinath, one of the most important pilgrim sites of Nepal for Buddhists and Hindus, sits on the floor of the valley with a backdrop of rugged snow-capped mountains. This place of peace and harmony is shared by devotees of two world religions. A local Nepalese explained that it is the only place on earth where you can find all five elements of which the universe is made, fire, water, sky, earth and air. He pointed me to the small ancient temple that every Hindu and Buddhist pilgrim visits. I loved Muktinath for its peaceful, gentle people, unhurried movement, prayer wheels spinning, and prayer flags flapping quietly in the breeze.

I planned to climb out of the valley the next day, but hadn't been able to find the trail. That evening as I sat in the warm, but smoky, comfort of the 300-year-old guesthouse, I wondered how I would manage to find my way to my next destination. Two British backpackers sat at the table drinking Tibetan tea. Both appeared weary but very fit. The taller of the two had a reddish face and spoke with a tired smile. He told me they'd spent three days in Muktinath.

"Where are you heading next?" he asked.

"Tomorrow, I plan to head through the Pass to Thorong Phedi."

They stared at me quizzically. "We heard from some Americans that the Pass is closed. They managed to get through, but it was a hell of a struggle."

"Oh, I guess I'll wait until it opens."

"That may take days. You can never predict the weather up there. What made you choose to do the trek clockwise? All the tour companies travel anticlockwise. We've been on the trail for fifteen days now and haven't met anybody travelling the opposite direction. The advantage is, you can spend a few days resting and acclimatising at Thorong Phedi or Letdor before the climb through the Pass. The Pass is much easier to negotiate on the Eastern side. If you climb from this side, you have to manage over 2000 metres in one day. It's very hard on the body and the lungs. You don't want to end up with altitude sickness, HAPE — High Altitude Pulmonary Edema. Once you start coughing up yellow phlegm, you need to get off the mountain as quickly as possible, or your lungs continue to fill up and you end up drowning."

I laughed. "I'm certainly not going to retrace my route and tackle it the other way." The laugh hid my sudden concern. I couldn't remember any hikers walking the trail clockwise. This was new information, including the fact that a 2000 vertical metre climb had to be negotiated to reach the Pass. I was aware of HAPE, but their reminder of the symptoms was not something I wanted to hear right then.

After chatting about my experiences with Land Drover transport and mule trains, I headed off to find a guide. Chandra, a bright-eyed Nepalese with olive skin and beautiful white teeth, was not hard to find. His name meant moon, and he wore a religious brass pendant around his neck. Chandra confirmed that the Pass was closed. I told him where I was staying and asked him to let me know when it opened. He asked for seven dollars to take me to the Pass, after which it would be relatively easy for me to find the next village.

Early that evening, Chandra called to let me know that the Pass was possible. We would need to leave at five in the morning to reach it by midday, otherwise it would be difficult to reach the next village before nightfall. I checked my gear, ensuring that my two torches with extra batteries were operational.

Chapter Twenty-Five - Frozen

"All that is gold does not glitter, not all those who wander are lost; the old that is strong does not wither, deep roots are not reached by the frost."
J. R. R. Tolkien

Early the next morning, I reluctantly removed my body from the warm sleeping bag and swallowed a bowl of rice. Then, while waiting in the dim light of the lodge's common area, I chewed a clove of garlic and washed it down with a glass of water. Chandra appeared on the stroke of five and led the way to the trail, which soon disappeared.

My torch gave me security as we commenced our climb out of the valley. Chandra didn't use a torch, so I figured he must have had excellent night vision. But an hour after leaving the village, my torch gave out, and the replacement batteries soon faded. Maybe the cold sucked them dry. I wondered how long they'd sat on the shelf in the store before I purchased them. Someone told me that batteries are like bodies, the higher the altitude, the quicker they're drained of energy. I'm not sure if that's true or not.

Now, plunged into darkness, I kept as close as I could to Chandra, not daring to stray from his footsteps. Eventually, the faint glow of the sun signalled the imminence of first light. I was thankful for my warm gear, my only concern being my hand-knitted gloves. The shop owner in Kathmandu had sold me the largest pair in the shop, but my hands matched the size of my feet, and a search for correctly fitting gloves had proved futile. The gloves stretched tight over my knuckles, the flesh clearly visible through the weave. Though adequate at the moment, I was in trouble if the temperature dropped any further.

I stumbled forward and kicked a rock a little larger than a cricket ball. It disappeared into the blackness. Seconds later, a crash sounded far below. I peered after it and realised that we walked on top of a narrow ridge with an almost fifty-metre vertical drop either side. The sun climbed into a cloudless sky, revealing towering ragged pinnacles, pointed skyward, and rich Rhododendron forests blazing in colourful contrast to the bare rocks. We stumbled over landslides of rocks of varying sizes — the mountains were alive with moving rocks — and we dodged many during the ascent, some the size of footballs.

At nine o'clock, we arrived at a small door-less hut, four metres square, used for emergency shelter, and Chandra suggested a break for ten minutes. I slung my backpack to the ground, took a drink from my flask, and minutes later, keen to get to the top as quickly as possible, I said, "Let's go."

The weather usually changed on the Muktinath side, the side from which we approached. If we made the Pass by midday, I should be clear to get to the next village before night. Chandra was exceptionally fit and, living at the altitude at Muktinath, managed breathing more efficiently than I could.

We walked on, and a saucer-shaped valley appeared, half a kilometre across. Chandra led the way through strange outcrops of rock that rose 200 metres from the valley floor. The top of the Pass came in sight, and with only 500 metres to go, my legs started to complain. Five centimetres of snow covered the ground, making the final climb to the Pass a greater challenge. Surprisingly, I made it with a reasonable amount of energy remaining.

The flat ground at the top was a welcome relief, and surrounded by snowy pinnacles piercing the cloudless sky, I stared in awe at the frozen wilderness.

Chandra smiled and thanked me for the seven dollars I placed into his hand. He was a great guide, leading the way, but with few words. He pointed ahead. "Follow this slope downhill, find the river and follow it. It will take you to Thorong Phedi."

I nodded and thanked him again, then watched Chandra disappear down the slope on his way back to Muktinath. Heart singing, I drank in the fresh crisp air at 5,400 metres. All I had to do was to walk downhill, find the river and follow it. I had all afternoon to walk fourteen kilometres — easy. I felt as if this were the best day of my life.

I commenced my descent and within minutes found the snow getting progressively deeper. *Just a deep drift. I'll be through it soon.* I ploughed on and on. The snow was soon up to my waist. If there was a track it certainly wasn't visible. I wondered if I'd moved off the higher ground. If so, I could've easily stepped into a hidden ravine covered by a thick layer of snow. I stopped and looked at my watch. One and a half hours had passed since I farewelled Chandra at the Pass. I estimated I'd descended no more than 500 metres. I had to press on. It *had* to become easier.

Ten minutes later, the temperature suddenly dropped. Clouds scuttled in and obscured the blue sky. It became cold — far too cold — and the serenity I'd carried up the mountain from the village vaporised. My stomach tightened. I was alone on the mountain. The sun disappeared, and the wind tore at my clothes. Menacing grey replaced the euphoria of a glistening panorama of sparkling snow and electric blue. The sting of wind-driven snow, my heavy feet and the burden of my backpack slowed me to a crawl. The wind grew to gale force, and I found myself standing rigid in a blizzard. I couldn't see a thing. I felt as if I were waist deep in snow, but when I looked down, I couldn't work out where the snow began. I'd never been in a whiteout before. What could I do? I couldn't just stand there. I fell onto my knees and started to crawl. Minutes later I got back to my feet and staggered forward. Again I fell to my knees and fought my way forward. Breathless, I stood once more and took another step forward. My right foot caught between rocks. I wrenched it forward and it flew out of my jogger. My backpack slid off my shoulders with alarming ease. I turned and plunged frantically into the soft snow, searching. At last, arms fully immersed, I felt it. I lifted my shoe above the snow and grappled with the laces, but I couldn't undo them — they were frozen. And I couldn't feel my hands — they, too, were frozen. Desperately, I tried to wrench my gloves free, but the sweat from my efforts had frozen them too. I smacked my hands together, over and over, and eventually movement returned to my fingers. I found my penknife and tried to cut the laces free. Finally, I achieved success, then I had to locate some string and thread the end through the eyelets. I leant back into the snow, lifted my frozen foot into the air and finally slid it into the wet shoe. It seemed to have taken forever to complete this simple task.

I checked my watch again. It had taken me an hour to advance 100 metres. I knew I wouldn't make it to the village. What should I do? I couldn't go forward; I couldn't go back. I didn't even know which way *was* back. In my efforts to restore my footwear, I'd lost direction. Everything was white. I couldn't see more than an arm's length in front of my face. No rocks, no landmarks. I staggered forward; hoping the effort of movement would provide warmth. Twenty paces further, I fell exhausted into the snow. I needed food. I searched in my pocket, but my fingers had frozen again. I couldn't feel a thing.

Smacking my hands together consumed more energy, but it broke the ice in my glove. I ripped my right glove off and flung it onto the snow in frustration, then I found a biscuit and stuffed it into my mouth. But there was no saliva in my mouth, and I choked trying to swallow the dry biscuit. Needing water, I reached for my bottle and found it frozen. I spat the biscuit onto the snow, then stared at it. It was the only thing I could see, but it indicated where the snow met the icy atmosphere. Dehydrated, I staggered forward and ended up crawling on my hands and knees, gulping for air like a person drowning. My heart felt as if it were going to explode. My right hand was frozen, and my backpack had been swapped for a bag of cement which crushed me into the ice. Tears ran down my cheeks, and I sobbed from deep within — wrenching, painful and uncontrollable sobs. *I can't go on. I have no strength. I want to sleep. I must sleep. What will Dad say? I won't make Latvia. I'll never see Margie again. I'm going to die.*

Eventually, I had no tears left. I lay motionless and exhausted, face flattened into the snow, feeling an icy hand grip the entire front of my body.

It may have been the release of the emotion. It may have been the motivating thought, *I've got to make it for Dad's sake.* It may have been my sheer determination to live, or my longing to see Margie, or likely all of those, but whatever the reason, energy slowly returned.

Get up. Keep your eyes open. And walk. Walk. I lifted my head and left two small indentations in the snow, marking the place that gathered my tears. Slowly, I managed to get upright. My breath turned to fog, and the wind instantly ripped it away. Like a drunk, I staggered forward, but I had no idea if I were headed the right way. I needed to return to Muktinath and quickly. But which way was back? I didn't even know up from down. I lurched forward and sensed I was going uphill. *That must be right.* I screamed at myself to keep going and said I could make it.

Finally, the wind eased, and I could see my breath billowing before me.

"Keep going. Keep going," I shouted.

The ache in my bare hand became unbearable. I unzipped my jacket and slid it inside. That gave some relief, but then I felt the cold on my chest.

"Keep going. You'll make it."

Suddenly, the fog lifted, and I saw the way ahead. I needed to change course by twenty degrees. Minutes later, the fog once again filled the air, and I staggered on. This experience repeated twice in the next thirty minutes, and each time I adjusted my direction.

"Thank you, God." I repeated. "Keep going; you can rest at the top," became my mantra. For the next half hour, I talked out loud to myself until, lungs bursting, legs screaming, body frozen, I finally reached the Pass. The claustrophobic fog cleared, and the wind dropped. I could breathe.

I stood there with tears of relief trickling into the snow. *There is a God.*

Black clouds still hung menacingly above the mountain peak, however, and there was no sun to warm my frozen body, nothing to penetrate the ice at my core. All was quiet, and the eerie wonderland appeared again. I decided to take a break — my reward. A loud clap of thunder broke the solitude. I jumped and glanced around. Was it thunder? No. A sheer wall of ice, half a kilometre high, sat above me, 200 metres wide, reflecting the afternoon sun. The sheet of glass hid a huge glacier — maybe 2000 tonnes — and it was on the move, inching its way forward, cracking.

If that breaks, I don't want to be standing here. I need to move fast.

There was no rest for me there. I broke into a run, accompanied by my visible breath and the sound of my feet pounding on the snowy carpet. *At least I'm alive.*

Fifteen minutes later, I looked back to the glacier and felt it was safe to stop. I needed fluid and found that the water in my bottle had melted a little. I even managed to wash down a wheaten biscuit. My watch told me it was three o'clock. I still had 2,000 metres to descend, and the sun would set at six.

When I got to the valley of rocky outcrops, I decided not to walk around them and the massive snowdrifts piled on their lower sides, as we did on the ascent, but to walk along the ridges to save time. I stepped onto the compacted snowy slopes and descended at speed, almost skiing. I completed four of these safely, but as I descended, the rocks become exposed. On the fifth descent — snow free, just tonnes of loose rocks — I lost my foothold and rolled to the bottom, frantically grasping for an anchor. Pain shot up my left leg. Had I broken it? I didn't think so, but it was very sore. I continued on, slipping and sliding, bringing rocks with me as I went down the mountain. The rocks became larger the further I descended, eventually becoming the size of houses. Desperate not to lose time, I continued to risk injury rather than walk around them.

The sun had set into half-light by the time I entered a dense pine forest that I hoped was near the village. The ground was so steep that I had to grip each tree to avoid slipping. I had no idea where I was going, but an hour later, the beautiful, welcoming lights of Muktinath appeared. My stomach called for soup, smoked goat, rice and tea, but I was prepared to eat horse or anything else I could sink my teeth into.

I drank four jugs of water to help my body recover from dehydration, then sat beside the fire, exhausted and grateful for the level of fitness I'd accumulated from years of football. Countless painful training sessions had kept me alive. Football matches that stretched me to breaking point, where every part of my being wanted to give up, had paid dividends. Without those years of physical and mental preparation, I would now be dead. I was pleased with my aerobic fitness, especially after I learnt that most travel groups carry oxygen, as a number of clients usually require it.

After dinner, I bumped into Chandra. He called in to the guesthouse to talk to an American couple. "You're back?" he said.

"I thought you were going on to Thorong Phedi?"

"Yeah, I was, but I struck a bit of bad weather."

Chapter Twenty-Six - "They've Done it Again"

"Never give up, for that is just the place and time the
tide will turn."
Harriet Beecher Stowe

I slept soundly that night. I don't think I moved a muscle, and my stomach screamed for food the moment I awoke. My breakfast increased twofold as the depleted cavity demanded replenishment. My concern then was for the fingers on my right hand. Though the colour had returned—it'd been a mix of purple and yellow when I'd gone to bed—the whole hand was numb. I mentioned this to one of the staff at the guesthouse, and he said, "You need to see a doctor as soon as possible. The closest doctor is in Jomson."

I sighed. My exhausted body then had to suffer a 30 kilometre trek with a heavy backpack.

Later that afternoon, I sat in front of the French doctor in Jomson. "There's nothing I can do for you," he said. "You'll not know for a few days if the damage is permanent. If your fingers turn black, you'll know it's permanent. Keep them warm and stimulated."

All I could do was hope for the best. I also took it as the excuse I needed for a rest day, which I spent soaking in the hot springs of Totopani.

* * *

The first item on my agenda on my return to Bangkok was a massage. A large sign in English attracted me to the front door of the shop in one of the back streets. A middle-aged woman ushered me into a large well-lit room with glass walls either side. Behind the glass sat at least twenty attractive Thai women wearing numbers.

"Which number would you like, sir?"

"I'll take number fifteen, please." I didn't mind.

The young woman left by a door at the rear of the room, while my hostess led me into a nicely-presented cubicle containing a double bed and mirrors around the walls. The young woman I'd selected appeared wearing undies and bra. The massage was worth every cent of the seven dollars. The long, firm strokes, the gentle manipulation of the tight knots and the aroma of the oil were all healing—an appropriate reward for my body after subjecting it to so much suffering over the previous weeks. A little slice of heaven! The only point of pain was my ribs, reminding me of my bruising encounter with the mule train.

When the girl finished, she asked, "Would you like something more?"

"Pardon?"

"Sir, would you like something more? It will only cost you a little extra."

"No, thanks. That's fine."

She looked down at the floor, hurt. "What's wrong with me?"

I lay there, thinking for a moment. I felt sorry for her. "I don't want anything else. You're very pretty. But that's all I want."

She nodded, and I slowly lifted my pampered body off the table.

My repatriation continued on Ko Samui Island. Every day, I swam in crystal-clear water, ate delicious seafood, watched the fishing boats return with their catch and slept. The feeling returned

230

to my hand on the last day. What a relief that was. (However, for the next twenty years, my hand always ached whenever I went skiing.)

Back in Bangkok, I checked in at the post office to see if Mum had sent any mail. Surprise! Two letters were handed to me. Sure enough, one was from Mum. I couldn't identify the writing on the other envelope and opened it, thinking it might be from one of my mates, but who?

Dear Peter,

I am writing to let you know that the house is being kept clean, the lawns mowed and Margie is taking good care of me ...

Who it was from? ... Beau, my dog! His paw print marked the bottom of the page! The letter gave me a brief update on what was happening around home. I laughed. Margie had gone to a lot of trouble to put the letter together, find an inkpad and persuade Beau to provide a paw print. This got me wondering. Did Margie have an interest in me that was more than that of a grateful tenant? Was this ghost-writing exercise a cover for an attraction to me? What was the latest in her relationship with the guy she was dating? He'd perceived me as a threat, not that I gave him any reason to think that way. Did he sense something from Margie that I'd missed? I didn't have any answers. But the letter gave me a lift.

Dad, Julie and Michael arrived in Bangkok on schedule. It was so good to see them. Dad managed the flight well, and his excitement showed in the way he enthusiastically updated me with news from home. He wasn't usually that talkative! To meet Julie's expectations, I moved from my two dollar-a-night accommodation in a back street of Bangkok to a fifty dollar, expensive hotel in the main drag. I loved showing them the sights of the city for the next three days.

Our flight to Moscow unfolded without drama. Julie had meticulously seen to all the bookings and arrangements, and we felt relaxed and on a high after our reunion in Bangkok. Dad was poised, ready to fulfil his dream of seeing his brother and other members of his family, to wander the fields of his farm, sit in his favourite armchair and walk the streets of the Old City of Riga. Julie and Michael chatted happily about seeing Dad back with his family, and for me, having Dad back on Latvian soil was the fulfilment of my greatest dream. The synthesizer was hopefully safe in the cargo hold and would bring joy to our family and the local community.

The immigration hall in Moscow was smaller than the one I'd experienced six years previously, and few people loitered in the terminal as we walked to the counter and handed the official our passports. He checked the photographs with our faces.

"Mr Arnold Jirgens and Mr Peter Jirgens, you may enter. Mr Michael Evans and Mrs Julie Evans, you are not permitted to enter the country. You will need to take a return flight from Moscow," he said.

Julie and Michael's jaws dropped in shock. Completely dumbstruck, I looked at Dad, not sure if the words had fully registered with him. What was going on?

I decided to take the lead. "What's the problem?"

"Mr and Mrs Evans are not permitted to enter the Soviet Union. They must take a return flight."

The official handed back our passports and visas, and beckoned Dad and me through the gate. Exasperated, I looked back at the official, but he stood there unflinching. *I can't believe this?* Michael comforted Julie, now in tears, and she looked at me expectantly, but there was nothing I could do. The decision had been made. I couldn't argue with the official, it'd be futile. You don't win against the Soviets. The man became agitated and insisted that we move.

Anxious not to cause a scene, I hugged Julie and Michael, then walked through the gate with Dad. It felt like a bad dream. I couldn't understand why only Dad and I were able to enter. My suspicious mind went to the darkest place. I thought they might be going to detain Dad and possibly me too. Perhaps they discovered that Dad fought against them with the Americans in the war, or maybe they checked the records from 1980 and realized that I'd flown under the radar back then. They gave no reason, no explanation as to why we were allowed into the country and not my sister and her husband. What would happen to Michael and Julie's bookings? I wondered. That dreaded knot tightened in my stomach again. The Soviets were still unquestionably in charge. So much for thinking the control has been relaxed! I wondered what else it meant for Dad and me. What lay ahead?

The main railway station at Riga witnessed an emotional reunion. Dad embraced his brother as I stood with tears streaming down my face. What a moment. Dad had waited impatiently for decades for this day. Dad was not one to show emotion, but he did that day. Uncle John was so pleased we'd made it, though distressed to hear that Julie and Michael had been refused entry. While he wasn't able to give a reason for the Soviet's decision, he didn't believe there was anything for us to be too alarmed about. However, he said, "You can never trust the Soviets. They can change their mind without warning." How true was that!

Herrings, smoked chicken, kotletes (meat patties), soup, potato pancakes, and rasols — a potato salad with eggs, gherkins, sausage and spices — lay ready on the table for our celebratory reunion. My cousin Peter provided some lively music on his piano accordion, while Dad and Uncle John laughed and joked. I loved watching them talk, even though I understood very little. Their faces and mannerisms said it all. This was a day they'd both dreamed about. The synthesiser was unpacked, and Dad gave a demonstration. Everyone clapped and cheered. My cousin picked it up and after ten minutes of experimentation played a simple tune. What a talented guy! John and Peter loved the synthesiser.

Dad said, "John can't wait to show it off to local band, he's excited. Tomorrow we go to office and pay duty."

Dad and Uncle John talked well into the night.

Next morning, porridge, omelette and rye bread prepared me for a day I'd never forget. Dad was keen to go to the office and pay the duty for the synthesizer. He wanted to pay it and get it out of the way.

Armed with US$1,200 and the stamped papers detailing the approval of the synthesizer, we headed for the duty office, while Dad and Uncle John discussed where they'd go after paying the duty. I knew Dad was itching to walk the streets of Old Riga, and I wanted to hear his stories of what it was like in his childhood.

I stood with Dad while Uncle John walked up the steps of the duty office and into the crowded waiting area. After a while, he walked down again, a frown creasing his forehead. "The Soviets are now demanding US$8,000," he said with a sigh.

Dad looked at me, speechless.

I shook my head, dumbstruck. "US$8000, that's ridiculous. Why have they raised it? They told us US$1,200 in Australia, and that's exorbitant enough."

Uncle John said something and turned to me. Dad interpreted: "He says you can't argue with them."

I'd heard that many times before. Here again, the Soviets were playing with their subjects, squeezing the life out of them. My chest tightened with anger. We sat in the house that afternoon in disbelief. Long periods of silence passed, each of us quietly staring into space. None of us wanted to explore Old Riga as we'd planned. The immediate decision was to return the synthesizer to Australia. US$8,000 was out of the question.

As the week progressed, discussion swung around to a plot to enable my cousin to keep it. My uncle didn't have 8,000 US dollars, nor did we. We'd brought around 1,200 dollars US in cash, but it fell far short of what the Soviets demanded. My uncle went back day after day, trying to negotiate the price down, but they wouldn't budge.

What were we going to do about the 8,000 US dollars import duty? After three or four days, it suddenly dawned on me that we might be able to use the black market. My uncle didn't have any experience in that area, because he'd never owned hard currency, but I'd increased my travel dollars in 1980 using this underground activity. The issue became, 'would the authorities accept Russian roubles instead of US dollars?' Buying goods with US currency and then selling them to locals on the black market in exchange for roubles would create the profit. My uncle returned to the administration office again and explained it was not possible to provide US dollars, as his family only had roubles. He returned with a smile on his face and said they would accept payment in Russian currency. Our spirits soared. The next challenge was to earn 8,000 roubles from our 1,200 US dollars. At this point, however, Dad and my uncle became anxious.

"What's up, Dad?" I asked.

"Your uncle saying, "I've been to Siberia twice, and don't want to go again. Don't think this a good idea — too risky. I not want to attract attention to me either. You can't trust Soviets. Let's take synthesizer back.""

I heard the concern in his voice and saw the anxiety on Uncle's face, but I was sure we could pull it off. I needed to be respectful of their concern but also confident and persuasive.

I reassured him that there would be no problems. My previous experience with the black market in Moscow had presented no difficulties. It took time, but gradually, a little ray of hope appeared. On reflection, I don't think I fully understood the degree of fear that arose for my family or anyone living in Soviet-controlled territory from walking close to the line. Also, my uncle didn't want us to get into any trouble, and again he tried to persuade me to take the instrument back to Australia. Repeatedly, I reassured him that all would be well, and since we'd gone to the trouble of bringing it into Latvia, I was determined to give the black market a go. The synthesizer was not going back to Australia, and that was that! My assertiveness won the day. Finally, Uncle John and Dad agreed.

So my cousin Peter, his friend and I headed off for our first hit on a Beryozka store. My cousin's Uncle , Imants was one of the few Latvians who owned a car. First, we looked at Japanese folding umbrellas in a variety of colours. They were selling for five US dollars. The standard issue of a Russian umbrella was black and four foot long. We reminded ourselves that everything we bought needed to be sold for at least eight times the purchase price if we were going to be successful in reaching 8,000 roubles. Beautiful Norwegian scarves caught our eye. Russian scarves were like sandpaper on your neck, but Norwegian scarves were soft and warm. Radial tyres were plentiful. In the Russian stores, you might wait six months for a tyre, if you were lucky, but the Beryozka shop had dozens. I made a list of the goods I believed we could sell quickly and get at least eight times their value. Uncle John and the family then went out and checked the price locals would pay for each item.

Research complete, we sprang into action. Over the next four days, we left various Beryozka shops with 300 dollars' worth of Japanese umbrellas, 200 dollars' worth of Norwegian scarves, and ten radial car tyres. I rolled two car tyres at a time through the checkout and into the boot of our waiting car. The car then drove off to contact a prearranged buyer, and I moved to the next shop to avoid suspicion. We repeated the process many times. It went well, so much so that we had roubles left over. On the last day, while we waited anxiously outside, my uncle cautiously entered the administration building with 8,000 roubles in his coat pocket. Would they go back on their word or raise the duty further? Anything was possible. Nothing was certain behind the Iron Curtain. Soon Uncle John emerged and showed us the stamped import docket. We were so pleased and relieved 'Operation Black Market' was over. Celebrations followed for the remainder of the day. My cousin became an instant celebrity. Most Latvians had never heard a synthesizer before, and to hear the music Peter produced amazed the locals. He was a talented one man band.

Dad and I returned to the administration office the following day to see if a permit had been granted to visit his family home and the farm, fifteen kilometres outside Riga. Now that the Soviets were relaxing control of the Baltic States, we had a chance. But our experiences up to that point of their abuse of Latvians had given us little hope — first Michael and Julie being turned back after being given approval in Australia, and then the inflation of the synthesizer duty. We'd submitted the completed form two days previously.

When I saw Dad walk slowly back from the counter, I knew instantly that the news was not good. He desperately longed to see the old place again, the home of his boyhood and early manhood. The place where he'd been accepted, secure, successful and at peace. The painful discrimination he endured in Nowra, the cruel failure of his business, left him feeling as though every bone in his body was out of joint. He didn't fit in Australia. He was Latvian and wanted to die Latvian. He lived with that agony; I lived with his agony.

"They're not going to issue a permit," he said with a sob.

I wanted to hug him, but he'd feel embarrassed, so I took a deep breath and swallowed my frustration. I wanted to scream. There was no good reason for the Soviets to continue their bloody game-playing. Cracks had appeared in their quest for power. Their iron grip was weakening and here, it seemed, was a pathetic, last-ditch attempt to assert their authority.

I put my hand on Dad's shoulder as we walked down the steps of the office. I didn't know what to say. In that moment of disappointment and anger, I silently resolved to find a way to reunite him with his farm, even if it killed me. Our visit was bitter sweet: so much laughter and celebration, so much disappointment.

Chapter Twenty-Seven - Walking Together

"An army of the people is invincible!"
Mao Tse-tung, Quotations from Chairman Mao Tse-Tung

Dad and Uncle John were eager to walk the streets of Riga, especially the Old City. We found our way to Lenin Street, to the statue of Lenin, which greets visitors as they enter the main artery of the city. A little further, on the right, just past the Planetarium, the statue in honour of the National Poet Rainis sits thoughtfully in open parklands known as Communards Square. Janis Rainis was Latvia's great poet. We wandered the grounds and stopped by the graves of twenty-seven Soviet Communards killed by Latvians in 1919.

"Who were the Communards?" I asked.

"Radical Communist youth group — very dedicated to Marx's ideas," Dad replied.

"Did you know your grandfather is buried here?" Dad asked, pointing to headstones set in the manicured lawn.

"Really?" This was part of our family history I knew nothing about. "How? Why?" Dad was more than happy to tell me. Dad thought carefully and spoke slowly. He always had trouble with English.

"Back in 1914 at outbreak of World War 1, Latvia still a province of the Russian Empire with no freedom — no special rights. Latvia helped Russia fight Germany. So did Lithuanians and the Estonians. They feared Germans more than Russians. Later, Russia pleased to help Latvia when we wanted to make our own national regiments. Our Latvians fighters—very fierce. Later, German Field Marshal von Hindenburg said he would've taken Riga by Easter 1916 if not been for the 'eight bright stars in the sky'—the eight Latvian Rifle Regiments." Dad moved his gaze from his feet and made eye contact with me. I loved these times when Dad became animated. I longed to hear the passion in his voice. He came alive. I gave Dad my total attention, surprised at how much detail he remembered.

"Russia gave in to Germany and Russian government lost direction after the Tsar stood down from the throne in March 1917. This made Latvia keen to set up its own independent State. Lenin deceived a group of Latvians including the riflemen with false promises—to help Latvia. He wanted them to join Red Army. My father, one of them. They joined Red Army and fought against 'White' Russian forces during Civil War. They helped Lenin set up a ... what do you call it ... puppet Soviet government in Latvia. They supported Red Army's capture of Riga in December 1918."

"Who were the White Russians?" I asked.

"White Russians—forces led by Lenin and the Bolsheviks called The Reds, the colour of revolution. The opposite forces called 'The Whites'.

Dad continued. "Latvian nationalists didn't like Bolshevik plans for Russia and Latvia. They not trust Lenin. They elected their first National Council—told Russians of their plan to set up independent State, separate from Russia. Of course, continuing conflict between National Council and puppet Soviet Government. At last, Latvian forces set Riga free in May 1919. Russian Communards died in this battle. Latvian Riflemen ... they switched sides because not happy with the Bolsheviks and realised Lenin

240

had tricked them. They then dedicated to fighting for freedom of Latvia and were killed." Dad's voice dropped as he finished his sentence. Sadness touched his voice. "Yes, your grandfather was one of the Riflemen." Then, after a long pause, he said, "By end of November, all German and White Russian forces left Latvia."

"Amazing," I whispered. I felt as if I were standing on sacred ground.

Dad and Uncle John stepped forward, closer to the graves. I gave them time alone with their memories.

Further down Lenin Street, we stood at the foot of the forty-two metre Freedom Monument made from granite, travertine and copper in the centre of Riga. It was a landmark for the city and a focal point for national celebrations.

I looked up at the slender figure of a woman lifting three golden stars towards the heavens. She stood proudly on a vertical column of white granite.

"What's the story behind the monument?" I asked. I could see Dad was glad I asked. He was more communicative and animated in his beloved country.

"Let's hide from the sun," he said and led us to some trees on the edge of the square. "Well, Peter," he began, once we'd settled on the grass, "on 27th July, 1922, after Latvia gained independence, calls were made for building a monument to commemorate the heroes killed in action during the War for Freedom. The proposal was a twenty-seven metre high obelisk, but the committee that the government set up to administer the project rejected the first design because artistically it wasn't up to the mark. During the Tsarist times, the main monuments were devoted to the Tsarist regime, such as the Victory Column in Riga Palace Square and the statue of Peter 1 in Alexander Boulevard." Dad pointed in their direction.

"The statue of Peter the First, built in 1910, commemorated the capture of Riga in 1710. Zhan Nicholas unveiled it, but the statue of Peter the First on his horse didn't last long. In 1915, because of the approaching German invaders, the statue was evacuated and placed on the ship *Seribino*, which was sunk by a German U-boat. The foundations of the statue remained, so the government chose it as the location for the new Monument of Freedom. Latvians wanted it to be something grander than the statue of Peter the First. It had to be honourable and express the idea of Latvian liberation. The government finally chose to erect a large vertical spire in three levels, decorated with many symbols of Latvia's past. You see here, Mother Latvia is holding three stars, Courland, Vidzeme and Latgalia, the three main Latvian regions. The unveiling took place in November 1935. I was only thirteen at the time and I remember it well. This place was full of cheering, patriotic people."

Uncle John spoke to Dad, and Dad smiled. "John wants me to tell you the rest of the story."

"Please do. I'm keen to learn." Dad was thoroughly enjoying himself, and I could see how much it meant to him. Here, on his turf, he was a different person, and I knew little of this man. I liked this part of my father, and it drew me to him.

"This monument stood strong during World War II. The Soviets and Nazi Germany tried to ignore it. Its location in the centre of the city made it difficult to remove silently. It would have caused an uprising by the locals. Most other pre-war monuments, especially in the countryside, were removed quietly during the night, but this was too large to simply take away. Then in 1949, the Council of the Peoples' Commissars of the Latvian SS proposed to restore the statue of Peter the First. While they didn't openly call for the removal of the Monument of Freedom, there was no other way to restore the statue of Peter the First on its historical location. The council decided at the end of the debate to reject the idea." Dad paused and smiled. "This next I like. It shows you how sneaky the communists are.

"A rumour circulated that the Russian artist Vera Mukhnia convinced the Soviets to keep the monument since it was of high artistic value. Also, the demolition might hurt the feelings of the Latvian people. Instead, the Soviets tried to reinterpret the meaning of the monument. The 'reinterpretation' described the Woman Statue not as Mother Latvia, but Mother Russia who holds three Baltic Soviet republics. Also, they tried to convince the people that the monument was erected after World War II." Dad laughed and looked at his brother. Speaking to me, he said, "The Soviets must have thought we are a bunch of idiots!"

I thought again of my kind Muscovite friend in 1980, brainwashed by the Soviets into believing that Russia had invented the telephone, cars and electricity. You could never believe what a communist says.

Dad continued. "Our people would have none of it. Obvious lies could not wash away the truth. For many decades, Soviet KGB recorded dozens of people placing flowers to commemorate independent Latvia. In 1963, the idea of demolishing the monument was raised again, but rejected because of fears of a negative response from our people. You can see how the Soviets have placed a trolleybus depot around the monument to prevent people from accessing it. Even though we can't touch it, it's part of us. Many folk come and stand here and remember what it stands for. If the Soviets tore this down, I think the country would rise up in revolt."

Dad and Uncle chatted for a minute while I took in the beauty and meaning of this artistic masterpiece. Mother Latvia, crafted from green stone, sat atop a solid column firmly anchored to the ground. The three golden stars of equal size that she held high sparkled in the sunlight, a true reflection of the Latvia of which I was a part; Latvia, which has survived occupation and oppression; Latvia, a land and a people, beautiful. Standing there beneath the monument, I felt proud to be Latvian.

Arnold Jirgens sugar cane cutting in Innisfail when he first came to Australia after WWII.

Arnold Jirgens and his sons John and Peter.

Milton, 1965: Arnold Jirgens' hard rock crushing plant.

Munich, 1980: Peter, seated right front, playing an English-man in Lilly Marlane.

Riga1986: Grandmother's grave site. Peter Jirgens (Peter's cous-in), Inara Jirgens (Auntie), Arnold Jirgens (father), John Jirgens (uncle), Peter Jirgens

Australia 1991: Margie, Peter, Beau (dog) and Anthea

Building Arnold Jirgens' coffin in his garage with his tools.
Left to Right; Tim Jirgens (grandson), Peter Jirgens (son), Peter
Jirgens (grandson)

2013: Julie & Peter Jirgens putting Arnold's ashes in his grandmother's grave.

2016: Author David Kerr with Peter Jirgens

Chapter Twenty-Eight - "She Loves Me, She Loves Me Not?"

"Love cannot pain, desire can."
Nilesh Rathod, Destiny of Shattered Dreams."

At this point, I'd been gone from Australia for three months, and I'd had no letter, no communication from anyone, including my dog Beau, after Bangkok. While my adventures demanded my full attention, a day never passed without me thinking of Margie. Sitting on the plane on the way home, watching Dad nodding off to sleep, my mind again drifted to what might happen when I walked through my front door.

Her boyfriend, if that was the right term, had seemed very keen. He worked overtime to impress — nothing subtle about his intentions. On the other hand, Margie played it cool and kept him and everyone else, including me, guessing. Margie was attractive, confident, practical, and intelligent, with a beautiful effervescence and spontaneity that drew people to her. I loved being around her, and I missed her. *In three months, anything can happen. She might be engaged or the relationship finished.*

John picked Dad and me up from the airport. John made no comment about Margie but said he called in on the house a few times and all seemed to be in order. I was hesitant to ask him how she was. Showing any kind of interest would give him ammunition to stir me with at a later date. I had to wait. All would be revealed soon. My excitement and anxiety increased as we approached home.

I opened my door to an immaculate house with freshly cut flowers on the dining room table. Beau gave me a slobbery welcome and, after a great deal of patting and romping, followed me around as I settled back in. The time for Margie to return from work approached, and I waited with an eye on the door.

Eventually, a car drove up and the engine stopped. I listened to her footsteps on the path, and when the door finally opened, my heart leaped.

Margie walked through the door, saw me and smiled. "You look well, Peter. It's so good to see you."

I stood and walked towards her, wanting to gather her in my arms, but holding myself back. "It's great to see you, too. Thanks for keeping the place so well." She seemed genuinely pleased to see me. I noted that my heart rate had increased since she'd appeared.

Her eyes sparkled. "I've cooked something special for you tonight, slow cooked lamb."

"Wow. That's great. Thanks." I couldn't have hoped for a better start.

Over dinner and until late, we talked about Margie's work and my adventures. She made no mention of a certain individual. Had she given him the flick?

By midnight, my eyes were falling out of my head. It'd been a long flight and a long day, but one I treasure. Reluctantly, I wished her goodnight, and she closed the door to her room. It was the best homecoming.

The following night, I cooked and continued with my travel tales. Margie appeared truly interested, but a knock at the door interrupted my storytelling. Margie jumped up and answered the door. It appeared that she was expecting someone. A man's voice came from the doorway, and minutes later my 'generous' party-giver, Margie's man of the moment, stood in front of me, reluctantly shaking my hand. After a brief greeting, Margie and this character disappeared into her room, and I sat stunned and deflated on the chair. *What a fool I am.* I'd been thinking that I'd caught Margie's eye. An hour passed and the murmur of voices continued. Feeling gutted, I retreated to my bedroom. My world was shattered, and I lay awake nursing my brokenness.

After a fitful sleep, I decided not to just lie down and give up. I sensed that Margie was interested in me but unsure of how deep it went. 'Never say die' was my motto in my childhood, the sporting field and the Annapurna Trail. I wasn't going to let her go without a fight.

My concern was the considerable weight I'd gained, weighing in at 105 kilos. I needed to lose it and fast. Football had been my weight regulator and, of course, I'd removed that from my schedule to go overseas. Running, I decided, was the cure, and it needed to be a marathon, something never attempted before.

I read Robert De Castella's book, and he advised six months of training in preparation. The event I chose was only three months away. I conscientiously began my training, and part of the regime was to fast for three days every three weeks. I was astonished at how aware I became after a three day fast. My senses became razor-sharp, and I wondered if hunger sharpened our ancient forefathers, who relied on their hunting skills to survive. In training for that marathon, I ran an over seven and a half kilometre circuit around local streets. My diet consisted of water. The following day, I repeated the effort and improved my time. On the third and final day of the fast, I ran the same distance in an even better time. It's incredible what the body can do! I was determined to shed the weight and look my best. I didn't want excess fat to lose the possibility of a relationship with Margie.

Then something amazing happened. Margie observed me returning, exhausted but exhilarated after my training, and decided to join me. As the sound of our joggers pounding the pavement moved into a synchronised rhythm, so our interests, thoughts and feelings became united. We talked together, cooked together, and laughed together. We fell in love. Unbeknown to me, Margie was having second thoughts about her boyfriend. She found ending the relationship a challenge and only achieved it after considerable struggle. Our lives continued to flow together, and we married on 7th May, 1988.

* * *

The visit to Latvia in 1986 achieved more than reconnecting Dad with his brother and family. It was a catalyst that, strangely, contributed to bringing Margie and me together. Also, it improved my relationship with Dad. He didn't say it, but he seemed proud that I'd taken the initiative in working the black market to create the funds to pay the duty for the synthesizer. He relied on me for the knowledge and experience I'd gained from travel. Conversation with him was now more relaxed and flowed easily. The opportunity to see Dad in his home environment had been the key. After that, I understood him.

But an ache continued for him, and for me. He wanted to return to his farm in Riga, to revisit the place of his birth and childhood, before he died. He longed to show his children the fields where he played as a child, the lake, and the old farmhouse. Dad had been deeply distressed that Julie and Michael had not been permitted into Riga in 1986 and was determined to ensure all his family would have the freedom to visit next time.

My visit with Dad had triggered more memories from his youth, of the hot summers, icy winters, music festivals and family celebrations. Letters from Uncle John kept him updated with family happenings, and the *Baltic Times* with political events. As the months went by, his longing grew stronger.

Chapter Twenty-Nine - The Healing

"There is nothing like returning to a place that
remains unchanged to find the ways in which you
yourself have altered."
Nelson Mandela

The March 1988 copy of the *Baltic Times* bore a page three head-
line, *Latvia: The Forgotten Land.* Dad finished reading the article
and handed the paper to me. The article reported the impassioned
plea of a twenty-two year old Australian journalist, Rolands Silaraups. He stated, "Australian journalists and private tourists
should now visit Latvia—and stay long enough to witness the
human rights breaches by the Soviets." Silaraups visited Latvia,
and on June 14, 1987, he defied Soviet authorities and led 5000
Latvians to a protest meeting at the Statue of Liberty in Riga. The
Russians brought thousands of their own policemen. The Soviets
expelled him in July 1987. Silaraups said he would continue the
fight against Soviet policy of russification and that "Gorbachev is
out to stamp out the national identity, culture and language for
all time." Other voices joined Silaraups protesting the ongoing
mistreatment of Latvians, Estonians, and Lithuanians. Under
mounting world pressure, Gorbachev released 200 prisoners of
conscience in June 1987, and the world celebrated. The West
asked, "What about the rest—454, imprisoned without guilt?"

Photocopying machines were still banned and there were still literature restrictions.

"Thought things getting easier," Dad said sadly. "Don't think we think about return trip yet."

I could hear the disappointment in his voice, and it echoed my own frustration. "Well, let's not give up hope. I'm sure the time will come," I reassured him. But time was running out. Dad was fit and strong, but I wanted a date to be set, and soon. My spirit will not rest until we return and Dad is reunited with his farm and family.

In November the following year, the Berlin Wall came down, and the West celebrated, but not as much as the millions who'd survived the brutal years of Soviet Communism. In December of that year, 1989, Dad talked seriously about returning to Riga to see the farm. The Baltic States were not free of the Soviet military. The Soviets tried to keep Riga in their iron grip, but their strength was waning. The Helsinki '86 group, which monitored the transgressions of the Soviets, was growing and launched a protest of hundreds of cyclists at the Monument of Freedom. Latvia was getting organised for a final showdown to reclaim their independence.

The groundswell of Latvian nationalism was met with a strengthening resolve by Soviet authorities to hold Latvia and its sister states in its clutches. The major concern was the power of OMON, Militsiya Special Purpose Unit, created by the Soviets. The Riga unit, created in 1988, was 'officially' designed to combat organised crime and support Soviet police. However, this heavily equipped fanatical group, also called 'the black berets', was dedicated to protecting Soviet order. Their brutal, criminal presence grew as Latvians united their voice for independence. Dad was aware of their growing threat. His heart ached for his beloved Latvia, but it was still not safe to go.

Early in 1989, Dad received an update from his brother.

The bad news was the growing threat of OMON. In the previous month, Latvia had declared its independence from the Soviet state. Uncle explained that Latvian radicals maintained ongoing demonstrations and were prepared to risk civil disobedience. The moderates, the Peoples' Front, achieved success democratically, through elections for the Supreme Soviet of Latvian SSR. Even though many Russians were strategically planted to Russify the country, especially in Riga, the Latvians had secured a clear major-ity on the council[4]. Their first priority was the restoration of the Latvian flag. However, Gorbachev was walking a tightrope, waving the 'perestroika' flag to the US and the West while facing tough criticism from the hardliners in Moscow. The Soviet resistance was being expressed through the five OMON groups, one of which was growing in strength in Riga. Unexplained disappearance of Latvian nationalists occurred, threats and strong-arm tactics by OMON. Tension was rising in Riga. Correspondence between Uncle John and Dad increased, giving details of the desperate Soviet efforts to maintain control over Latvia and her two sister states. The air of uncertainty hung in the air at home whenever Latvia was mentioned in the media. Uncle John's letters were quickly opened when they arrived, Dad desperate to learn if his brother and family were safe.

The letter that created a celebration came in March of 1991. We'd heard on the news of the uprising in Latvia and the military response of the Soviet army. On May 4, 1990, Latvia began a path to full independence from the Soviet Union. Soviet officials in Moscow and their supporters in Latvia tried to halt the Latvian fight for further independence by bloody provocations. Blood flowed in Vilnius, a neighbouring city, but the Soviet government wanted to avoid a repeat of the killings in Riga. Fearing an attack from Soviet tanks, 250,000 Latvians flooded Riga. It was to be a peaceful protest, but it didn't happen. Janis, my cousin, heard sporadic gunfire throughout the nights. The flood of people from the countryside created significant challenges. Janis said it was a massive task to feed the protesters, and they spent many nights suffering in the cold, defending their blockades. The barricades were made from any materials on hand, blocks, farm machinery, tractors and woodcuts. The protesters demolished a three-storey wooden house to provide barricades in the streets to make a statement to the Soviets, who'd surrounded the city with thousands of troops.

Not only were the streets blockaded. Barricades surrounded the entire Old City. The people piled all government buildings high with obstacles. Soviet tanks could've easily crushed the barricades, but such action would result in reactions from the West. The United States and the West were busy with the Gulf war. Riga, filled with Western journalists, watched the events in Latvia closely. Two cameramen in Riga were killed. Both filmed their own deaths as bullets hit them. Two militia officers died. These bloody shootings strengthened the condemnations of the international community. Soon after this, many of the barricades were removed.

The times of the barricades were legendary, a sign of never-before-seen unity of the Latvian people. People of all ages spent cold nights in the Old City to protect their leaders, ready to face tanks with empty hands, and prepared for military activity. Some had hunting rifles and World War II weapons, ready to fight. The Soviet government was unable to face such a crowd with tanks; it would have resulted in a bloodbath larger than Vilnius. This was clear testimony that Latvians had the courage to fight for their freedom at a critical time in their history. If Dad had been in Riga at the time, he would have been there[5].

Sadly, it was not possible to leave Australia to join the celebrations of the new Latvia. Another five years passed before Dad's dream came true. I put preparations in place in early June 1996, and Dad, John and I flew to Hamburg. We decided to hire a car and retrace Dad's steps around Germany after the war, where he spent twelve months selling cigarettes to the US troops on the black market. Dad loved reminiscing about these days of survival before he sailed in *The General Black* to Australia. John and I were intrigued by his ingenuity, daring and survival strategies.

The scene when we eventually arrived at Riga airport was a mixture of smiles and tears. Julie flew in from Australia; Uncle John drove from his home; and Dad, John and I touched down from Moscow. Conversation flowed freely as we made our way to a welcome dinner with the family. Uncle John's English had not improved, and we still relied on Dad to explain what was happening in the family and Riga. Though care and vigilance still had to be taken on the streets in Riga, the good news was greater freedom of travel within Latvia — no more permits! The celebrations with the family ran well into the night, and I found it difficult to switch off as I headed for bed. Tomorrow, the dream would finally be realised; we would see the farm.

The next day, Dad walked onto a paddock overgrown with weeds, his voice flowing with energy. "We had over 100 milking cows — needed housing four months of year." He proudly waved his outstretched hand. "I built ... ramp where our horse and cart reverse up ramp — we throw hay from cart to cattle." He nodded towards an old building. "See big shed. Put cows in for winter."

We walked on further, and Dad pointed to a tangled mass of trees, overgrown by weeds. "Here we had beautiful orchard — an acre of trees — provide us with fruit. Much of fruit preserved for eating in winter. A little further on, Dad said, "Now you see lake." A body of water the size of two tennis courts lay behind the cattle sheds.

"One of my jobs in winter, with brother John, saw blocks of ice from the lake. Lake freeze to depth of ... thirty centimetres. You see near lake, under old oak tree, ground falls sharply. We stack blocks of ice against sloping bank on three sides and cover with planks of wood. Then put down a layer of soil — make timber

259

door for front for entrance. This our cool room in hot months."

How ingenious. The outline of the area was still evident, even though it'd not been used for many years.

"When Russians took over after World War II," Dad continued, "everyone owned everything, and no one owned anything, three families lived in our house. No one care for our house — same for all places belonging to State. Now it's in bad way — very sad."

Dad was so proud of his place. He became animated as we walked over soil and floorboards that held so many memories. I expected him to be more despondent with the way the farm looked, its deterioration due to lack of care, but he seemed philosophical. I think Uncle John had prepared him for the worst.

We walked around the three-storey house built of solid stone with a terracotta roof. It contained twelve fireplaces, a cheese factory on the first floor and a section where Dad used to brew beer. I realised then the quality of life he once enjoyed. He was one of the tsars. In Australia, he saw himself as a struggler, a failure. The contrast was powerful, and I understood his pain and grief in being wrenched from the place he loved[6].

Our second time in Riga brought us even closer together, and me more firmly into Dad's world. His lifelong dream had finally been achieved. We spent time together wandering the cobblestones of the Old City of Riga, and sitting in the parks and by the canals[7]. Dad and Uncle John spent hours laughing and joking, catching up with old friends. It gave him a new lease of life.

When the final goodbye came and Dad and Uncle John faced each other, I sensed they both believed this was the final goodbye. They would not see each other again. Dad's hand trembled as he embraced his brother for the last time, and he blinked back tears as he turned to walk through the security gate at Riga airport. I struggled to manage my own emotions: sadness of leaving family, a city and a land I'd come to love; grateful for the privilege, for us as a family to share it with Dad; and relief that we left safe, without threat or challenge from the Soviet authorities. Mission accomplished.

The visit in 1996 was the final healing chapter in my relationship with Dad. Over the years, and it has been many years, I gradually accepted Dad. I matured as I gained an understanding of my own struggles. That visit was like a new shaft of light that cut through the clouds. A new living picture of his early life in Latvia emerged: a picture I could see, touch and smell. I understood the struggle and the success that followed. I made sense of the powerful impact of the war, which he spoke little about, especially the times of horror. I understood his struggle to settle in a foreign land. The discrimination, rife at the time in the '50s and '60s; his pain at being ripped off by his bank manager; his prolonged fight with the English language that left him partially socially isolated, contributed to his unsettledness. Dad was a clever man and able to speak four languages, but English was a stumbling block, and sometimes, even I could not understand him.

His grandchildren were unsure of him because of his accent and big bushy beard, and he seldom appeared relaxed with any of them. He didn't know what to do or say, and for any of them to sit on his knee was a rare moment of intimacy. He was more content with his own company and with the companionship of my mother. After he recovered from his huge debt, he bought a lease at Grawin, near Lightning Ridge. The ground was bare, but he loved it and spent slabs of time burrowing into the tough terrain. My mother hated the place at first, but he gradually seduced her by parking a caravan onsite, building a septic tank, shower, annex and stove. When he finally retired, he spent months tunnelling through the rock. He was as happy as a pig in mud. Now I understood and could say, 'I love you.'

Chapter Thirty - Ashes to Ashes

"Clay. It's rain, dead leaves, dust, all my dead ancestors.
Stones that have been ground into sand. Mud. The
whole cycle of life and death."
Martine Vermeulen

We assembled at Nowra Crematorium to say our final goodbye to Dad. It was a private service—just for the family. That's the way Dad wanted it. Tamara, Julie and Michael's daughter wore Latvian national dress, and my two sons, Campbell and Josiah, wore Latvian ties. Unfortunately, we didn't have a Latvian dress for my daughter Anthea. We believed it was important to include all the children in our farewell to Dad. The younger children were also present—John and Kathleen's sons Cohen, Peter and Timothy, and their daughter, Shon. Also, Julie and Michael's son, Haydn. Family members carried the casket into the chapel, with the knocker John and I had secured on the front knocking fittingly as we entered the door. We had a simple service. Michael, my brother-in-law, and I spoke of Dad's legacy to his family, and after the service we gathered for a wake at Julie's place at Riverview Road, where friends joined us. I was emotional, much more than I thought I would be. Mum had done much of her grieving as she watched Dad decline during the previous twelve months. But no matter how well you're prepared for the death of a loved one, it still comes as a blow. She was numb, and I had some catching up to do with my grief.

Julie's wishes were for half of Dad's ashes to be placed with his mother's casket in Riga. The other half to be kept for future consideration, knowing that Mum was still alive. With his ashes concealed in a small urn, Julie and I returned to Riga in 2013. My aunt and family gathered at the cemetery for a short service to place the ashes beside my grandmother's casket, part of the same plot, suffering the decay of time since she was buried in 1983. The sun shone down on our reverent gathering as the priest prayed, read from the Bible and spoke the words of the Committal.

My aunt, standing at my side, said, "Peter. Do you remember when you visited grandmother in 1980 and there were lots of tears? You had tears, she had tears."

"Yes," I replied. I remember it well.

"You gave her your hanky," my aunt continued.

"Did I? I don't remember that."

"Yes, and when you left she put it in her drawer and said she didn't want it washed, because it had your tears on it. She kept it in her drawer until a week before she died. She knew she was dying and she gave your hanky to her son and said, "This is my grandson's, and I want it placed with me in my coffin when I'm buried.""

Tears filled my eyes again, and I looked down at her coffin. "Poor grandmother."

Our small gathering slowly left the graveside, Dad's wishes now fulfilled. Born in Latvia and now ... forever in Latvia, at one with the soil he loved. The graveside was covered — ashes to ashes, dust to dust — where he always longed to be, embraced by the land he loved. United with the rich soil, which gave life to his forefathers, unified now with the earth, which provided him with both pain and pleasure. Now, no more struggle, only peace.

"We shall not cease from exploration
And the end of all our exploring
Will be to arrive where we started
And know the place for the first time."
T.S. Eliot, Four Quartets

Endnotes

1. My brother has done more practical work for them than most people I know in the region. Aboriginals had no employment and had significant social problems. John showed them how to price jobs and operate the machinery. He bought them a grader. They won a contract and have been working on the roads in Wreck Bay for many years. (Also, John hired a plane in 2008 to write 'sorry' in the sky over Sydney harbour on the reconciliation walk over the Harbour Bridge.)

2. Jack Gibson was a celebrated coach when I played first grade in Nowra. On many occasions he took struggling clubs to win grand finals. He was a genius, creative and willing to think outside the square. One of his masterful moves involved the five-eighth. Instead of passing the ball across the players to the winger, the five-eight would kick it direct to the winger, catching the opposing side off-guard. I thought our team could do the same move, except I would throw the ball instead of kick it. The play went like this. When the opposition put the ball out, it was our ball, ten metres in from the side line. Most of the opposing players would congregate ready for what they believed to be an offensive strike, noting the concentration of our players. Out on the opposite side line, our winger would crouch over, busily doing up his shoelaces, and behind him our burly fullback, fully alert, but seemingly

267

uninterested in the current proceedings. I'd then play the ball and 'dummy' to the blind side where the opposition believed the ball was going. As I threw the 'dummy', I adjusted my grip and torpedoed the ball to the other side of the field, where the winger was waiting. He passed it to the fullback who was running at full pace and could take the ball to the try line for an easy try. Our coach was nervous with this move, which we never overplayed, for if something went wrong, we were vulnerable and it could go badly against us. The first time we tried it, we were playing Kiama. After I threw the ball to the winger, it was passed to the fullback in full flight. One fast opponent took the fullback out, metres before the line, but not before he off-loaded it into my waiting hands, resulting in a try. Naturally we couldn't do this play often, as the word would get around. It was always fun when we ran with it. Great moves — great memories.

3. I had no idea of the extent of the horror of those years, 1940–1944. It was later in life when I read the speech by a ninety-five-year-old Russian writer, Daniel Granin. The chilling account of what happened on those streets will never leave me. Granin delivered his grim eyewitness account during a speech at a commemoration service for the victims of National Socialism on International Holocaust Memorial Day. This was held at the Reichstag building, seat of the German lower house of Parliament Bundestag, in Berlin on 27th January 2014.

    Granin's account of the devastating siege, during which up to 1,500,000 people perished, most from starvation, is detailed in the *Book of the Blockade*. The nearly two and a half year siege of Leningrad is perceived as one of the darkest moments in Russian history. It began in September 1941, three months after Nazi Germany launched its Operation Barbarossa invasion against the Soviet Union. Granin recounts:
    "The blockade was sudden and unexpected, as much as the

war itself was unexpected for the country. There were no reserves of fuel, no food … Then, one after another, disastrous events started to occur, power supplies were stopped, there was no water, no sewerage system operating, no central heating in place …

"Hitler planned to take Leningrad by forcing people to die of hunger, with the Nazis assuming starvation would prove to be the most effective weapon.

"Hitler ordered [his troops] not to enter the city to avoid losses in street battles, where tanks were unable to take part. German troops, in fact, comfortably and easily expected the coming famine and cold would force the city to surrender," Granin said.

"In reality, the war stopped being a war. From the enemy's side, it gradually turned into an expectation of surrender.

"Indeed, with the heating switched off during the bitterly cold winter at the beginning of the siege, from 1941 to 1942, thousands of residents of the former imperial capital died of hunger and exhaustion each day. Rations fell to just 125 grams of bread per person.

"People were forced to eat rats, cats, earth and glue. Some resorted to cannibalism,"

Granin told the parliament. He said he met a mother who fed her twelve-year-old daughter with the remains of her dead three-year-old daughter, to save at least one child. The writer recalled how dead bodies littered the streets of Leningrad for days, as the survivors were too weak to bury them.

4. Hundreds of thousands of Russians were sent to Latvia to live when Russia invaded Latvia after World War II. In an attempt to Russify the country, Soviets changed signs, including street signs, and insisted the Russian language was used in public. In 1991 after Russian control ended, Latvia changed the signage to reflect Latvian culture and the Latvian language replaced Russian in public. Latvians were fiercely dogmatic about re-establishing their language and culture.

After successive waves of oppression by foreign powers, they have been galvanised through the fire of persecution and suffering. Like other nationalities that have migrated to Australia and other lands, they have settled together for mutual support and security to celebrate their culture. Many Latvians settled in Melbourne, Adelaide and Sydney. During my employment with the council, I befriended a work colleague, Martin, who, in his boyhood, attended a Latvian school in Sydney on Saturday mornings, learning the language, songs and culture. I knew nothing about such schools. Our family lived in Nowra without the support of fellow Latvians. It was a lonely existence in many ways, but that is all we knew, and we managed. A few years ago before Mum died, John, Julie and I took Mum to the annual Latvian celebration in Sydney. Even though Mum was not Latvian, she embraced Dad's culture and family. There was much food, singing and dancing at the festival. She loved it and so did I. In Riga, every five years, they have a music festival of song and dance. During the previous four years, around two hundred thousand people submit their songs and music, and the number of participants for the festival is reduced to forty thousand. Singing and dancing is a central part of Latvian culture, which has been a powerful force to preserve the spirit and resolve of the people. Julie and I attended the festival in Riga in May 2013. We loved the atmosphere. Anywhere in Riga where there was a suitable setting, music of some description was happening. It culminated in a mass concert of Latvian choirs and dancing groups from around the world at the main stadium at the end of the Festival.

5. Dad spent a couple of years in Germany before he came to Australia, waiting to see what would eventuate in his homeland. On 20th March, 1948, he left Hamburg on a ship called

The General Black bound for Australia. The *General W.M. Black* was one of the most active ships of her type in the American navy, transporting troops after her commissioning in February 1944. She made many transpacific voyages, ferrying refugees to safe havens, including Australia. He was keen to fly to Hamburg, hire a car and then retrace his steps to Riga. When I knew he decided to revisit Riga, and see his farm, denied to him on his visit in 1986, I desperately wanted to join him, but had three small children and didn't want to borrow money. If a black market ran in Australia, I think I might have used it. I had to come up with a way to make some extra money and quickly. I had worked in the council in the previous three years as an engineer building roads. The idea of sealing driveways on rural properties was immediately planted, germinated, fertilised and watered all at once. Within twenty-four hours, I had a business card made up. The following afternoon after work, I drove around looking for property entrances where a firm layer of road base existed. I could more easily compact and seal these driveways for a price far less than using hotmix or concrete. So I said to my brother John and Dad that if I could raise the money in time I would join them. In the next three or four months, I shovelled sixty tonnes of coloured stone, manipulated trailers and machinery, collected an assortment of blisters and calluses and raised the required amount of money.

6. Dad received a letter from the Latvian government, advising he could have the land back. Dad happily gave his half to his brother.

7. The Germans established Riga in 1205. It was a great trading city and attracted invasions from the Vikings and other raiders intent to help themselves to the rich spoils of the city.

To protect themselves, they dug a canal around the old city. During my last visit to Riga in 2013, I kayaked the canal and marvelled at the enormous effort needed to move the many thousands of tonnes of soil and rock to create the moat. The canal measures around twenty metres wide, with a depth of two metres, created with the picks and shovels of the towns-people who slaved for two years. It is further testimony to the determination and strength of Latvians who were unwavering in the defence of their territory from stronger and more powerful nations. Whenever a community pulls together, anything is possible!

Latvia has survived and emerged stronger as a nation since its suffering in the grip of communism. I know Dad would have loved to have been part of the new era. As I freely walked around Riga in 2013, I could not help but see the contrast between my first visit in 1980 and following visits. A rich variety of colours replaced the common grey of the Soviet fashion houses. Plenty has replaced scarcity. Where there was fear and anxiety, now there was laughter and celebration. Slavery had made way for freedom. As I walked the streets of the Old City, I experienced a deep respect for my people and the way they survived those years of occupation. In 1980, I noticed the decline of the roadway over the canal. My 'engineering eyes' noticed the concrete cancer on the bridges because of the thickness of the concrete encasing the steel structure—only forty millimetres thick. The expansion and contraction of the steel because of the harsh weather had caused moisture to invade the structure. Eventually, the steel corrodes and the bridge needs to be replaced. The extreme temperatures required at least sixty millimetres. However, the Soviets had taken short cuts, and the results were obvious. I remember thinking at the time how costly the bridges would be to replace: millions of dollars. However, in recent visits I noticed they have all been reconstructed. They have found the resources, and a new Latvia is emerging. Latvia had successfully resisted and overcome every shortcut, every cost-cutting measure, every attempt to invade the Latvian mind and corrupt their culture.

A Note from the Author

If you enjoyed this book, please leave a review at your point of purchase. I would be very grateful, not only because I love to hear your opinion but also because your review will help other readers decide if they would like to read the book.

Find more great books from AIA Publishing at:
http://www.aiapublishing.com

Acknowledgments

I'm very grateful to Peter for his patience with me, for Peter McAra's inspiration and encouragement, and for Tahlia Newland's excellent editing skills and support.

Peter would like to acknowledge his sister Julie Jirgens, who read the manuscript a number of times and has ensured the accuracy of events, people and places. Further, in his words: "I am grateful to Dave for enabling this story to be told, and I'm sure that my father would be proud of this book. I'd like to thank David for his dedication, patience and insightfulness in writing and rewriting this book and Peter McAra, who was a great support and encouragement to Dave throughout this process."

About the Author

David Kerr is a relationship therapist, educator, radio broadcaster, pastor, traveller and artist. He has an M.A. (Theol) Sydney College of Divinity, majoring in Counselling and Christian Education, and other tertiary qualifications in Counselling, Religious Education, Divinity and Therapy.

David's journey has been shaped by issues of social justice, the impact of clients' experiences and the stories of fellow travellers, which feed his passion for writing. He is ready to leave this planet when he believes he can no longer make a difference.

This is his first book, and he enjoyed writing it so much that he is already working on his next one.